CRITICAL THINKING AND DEFENDING THE BIBLICAL WORLDVIEW

DR. JOE MANNING

Trilogy Christian Publishers
A Wholly Owned Subsidiary of Trinity Broadcasting Network
2442 Michelle Drive
Tustin, CA 92780

10 9 8 7 6 5 4 3 2 1
Library of Congress Cataloging-in-Publication Data is available.
ISBN 978-1-68556-248-9
ISBN 978-1-68556-249-6 (ebook)

DEDICATION

This book is dedicated to my wonderful wife of forty-six years, Gloria; my two daughters, Lisa and Tami; my son-in-law, Jason; and my two grandsons, Brady and Liam.

TABLE OF CONTENTS

PROLOGUE   07

PROLOGUE

You might be asking, "Why a book on critical thinking and the Bible?" Isn't critical thinking related to science and, therefore, according to the secularist, incompatible with the Bible? The answer to the first part of the question is yes, critical thinking is related to the field of science. Critical thinking involves constantly asking questions, examining information and evidence, and figuring out conclusions. All these actions are the basis for the scientific method, which then gives good evidence on which to base conclusions. However, the answer to the second part of the question is no; science and the Bible are not incompatible. Skills in critical thinking are vital for the Christian today as he encounters fallacious arguments raised against the truthfulness of the biblical worldview. Sadly, too many believers today are unprepared to respond to those arguments, challenges, and this is the reason for the writing of this book.

Fallacious arguments against the biblical worldview

abound in our culture today. As will be shown in this book, these arguments can be found in the news media, books, magazine articles, school classrooms, and in conversations with friends and family members. All too often, because the Christian is unprepared to respond, the argument is left unchallenged. The goal of this book is to help prepare the Christian to not only respond to the logical fallacy but to do so in a manner that may create an opportunity for sharing the gospel.

Chapter 1 provides the reader with an introduction to critical thinking. What is it? Why is it important for the Christian, and how will the skills of critical thinking help him in responding to fallacious arguments raised against the biblical worldview?

Chapter 2 will establish the biblical foundation for developing the skills of critical thinking. Some today believe that skills in critical thinking are not necessary; all that is needed is faith, but as will be demonstrated in this chapter, critical thinking and faith work hand in hand. The reader will be shown, using various passages of Scripture, that a fundamental part of his calling as a Christian is to demolish arguments and every pretension that sets itself up against the true knowledge of God. This is critical thinking and is a component of what it means to love God with all your mind.

Chapter 3 demonstrates the connection between critical

thinking and evangelism. Often, when attempting to share the gospel with a lost person, the Christian will encounter an unbeliever who needs help in overcoming obstacles to Christianity before his heart will be open to hearing the message of salvation. Those obstacles could be issues such as the problem of evil, the conflict between science and the Bible, and the Christian position on many of the social issues (abortion, homosexuality, same-sex marriage, transgenderism) within our culture today. It is here that the skills of critical thinking will aid the Christian in identifying the obstacle and formulating a response that may help in demolishing that stronghold and, in the process, open the heart of the person to hearing the message of the gospel. Several examples from the Bible and personal experiences will be shown to demonstrate how the skills of critical thinking can be used in evangelism.

In chapter 4, the reader is provided with a basic definition of a logical fallacy and shown how to identify its premises and conclusion. The final part of this chapter demonstrates to the reader how, through the asking of questions, to formulate a response to the argument in a manner that may create an opportunity for sharing the gospel.

Chapters 5 through 16 provide a description of twelve logical fallacies this writer has encountered while sharing the gospel. In these chapters, each of the fallacies is defined and illustrated using examples from real life, magazines, books, and the Bible. The reader is also shown how to respond to these fallacies in a way that may open the door for sharing more of the gospel's message.

The final chapter, chapter 17, provides a short summary and a list of websites where the reader may go to find more helpful resources to aid in his development of critical thinking skills.

Chapter 1

INTRODUCTION TO CRITICAL THINKING

———

C ritical thinking is defined as:

> ...the intellectually disciplined process of actively and skillfully conceptualizing, applying, analyzing, synthesizing, and/or evaluating information gathered from, or generated by, observation, experience, reflection, reasoning, or communication, as a guide to belief and action[1].

Robert Bowman defines critical thinking as "...the ability or skill to think in such a way as to form judgments, assessments, or evaluations of ideas, or claims, that will aid in the effort to arrive at a true understanding of those particular ideas or claims.[2]" According to Peter Kreeft, "Another word for 'critical thinking' is 'logical thinking.'"[3] He explains:

1 "What Is Critical Thinking?" University of Louisville, accessed January 10, 2020, http://louisville.edu/ideastoaction/about/criticalthinking/what.
2 Robert Bowman, "Lesson 2: Basic Principles of Critical Thinking," in Critical Thinking (Edmond: Credo House, 2019), digital audio recording.
3 Peter Kreeft, "Critical Thinking for Christians," Catholic Culture, accessed October 14, 2019, https://www.catholicculture.org/culture/library/

This is a high and holy thing, in fact a very Christian thing because the ultimate foundation of logic is the Logos, the eternal Mind or Reason or Inner Word of God, which John's Gospel identifies as the pre-incarnate Christ. The human art and science of logic is the instrument that teaches us to rightly order and structure our thoughts, as a means to the end of thoughts, which is truth[4].

Skills in critical thinking are tools for the Christian to employ when attempting to answer fallacious arguments raised against the validity and truthfulness of the biblical worldview. The goal of critical thinking is not to win arguments but to help an individual formulate a response through observation, experience, reflection, reasoning, and communication to the arguments raised against the gospel and to do so in such a manner that it may lead to an opportunity for sharing the good news of Jesus Christ.

Over the last few years, we have witnessed several self-professed Christian leaders state that they are walking away from the faith, one of which was Hillsong songwriter Marty Sampson[5]. In a July 2019 Instagram post, he gave his reasons:

view.cfm?recnum=9243.

4 Kreeft, "Critical Thinking."

5 A true believer in the Lord Jesus Christ cannot walk away from their faith; he is eternally secure in the hands of the Lord as stated in John 10:27–28, "My sheep hear My voice, and I know them, and they follow Me; and I give eternal life to them, and they will never perish; and no one will snatch them out of My hand." Jesus gives eternal life to the sheep,

"This is a soapbox moment so here I go. How many preachers fall? Many." He continued. "No one talks about it. How many miracles happen. Not many. No one talks about it. Why is the Bible full of contradictions? No one talks about it. How can God be love yet send four billion people to a place, all 'coz they don't believe? No one talks about it. Christians can be the most judgmental people on the planet—they can also be some of the most beautiful and loving people. But it's not for me[6]."

In a follow-up interview in August 2019 with CBN News, Sampson clarified his statement and provided further reasoning for his struggle with his faith:

If most of humankind had a choice, would we not rid the

---

true believers. There is no qualifier, such as if they remain faithful, in His statement that they will never perish. He further states that there is no one who can snatch them out of His hand; that includes themselves. The Apostle John states in 1 John 2:19, "They went out from us, but they were not really of us; for if they had been of us, they would have remained with us; but they went out, so that it would be shown that they all are not of us." The reason the "antichrists" left was to demonstrate that they were not true believers in God. True believers may experience periods of doubt and times of wandering in the wilderness, but they will never walk away from their faith in God. He knows how to rescue them. (2 Peter 2:9a, "Then the Lord knows how to rescue the godly from temptation, and to keep the unrighteous under punishment for the day of judgment.")

6 Leah MarieAnn Klett, "Hillsong writer reveals he's no longer a Christian: 'I'm genuinely losing my faith,'" The Christian Post, accessed July 27, 2019, https://www.christianpost.com/news/hillsong-writer-reveals-hes-no-longer-a-christian-im-genuinely-losing-my-faith.html.

world of the scourge of cancer? Or sickness and disease? Why doesn't God do such a thing? Of course there is an answer to this question, but the majority of a typical Christian's life is not spent considering these things. Questions such as these remain in the too hard basket[7].

Questions in the "too-hard basket" are often fallacious arguments raised against the Christian faith. By developing the skills of critical thinking, Christians can learn how to formulate stronger and more cohesive responses to these challenges and turn the questions in the "too-hard basket" into opportunities for sharing the gospel.

In a 1939 sermon titled "Learning in War-Time," C. S. Lewis spoke of the need for a more intellectual church. Lewis stated:

If all the world were Christian it might not matter if all the world were uneducated. But, as it is, a cultural life will exist outside the Church whether it exists inside or not. To be ignorant and simple now—not to be able to meet the enemies on their own ground—would be to throw down our weapons, and to betray our uneducated brethren who have, under

7 "Hillsong Leader Denies Renouncing Faith, but Says He's on Incredibly Shaky Ground," CBN News, accessed January 10, 2020, https://www1.cbn.com/cbnnews/entertainment/2019/august/hillsong-leader-denies-renouncing-faith-but-says-hes-on-incredibly-shaky-ground.

God, no defence [sic] but us against the intellectual attacks of the heathen. Good philosophy must exist, if for no other reason, because bad philosophy needs to be answered. The cool intellect must work not only against the cool intellect on the other side, but against the muddy heathen mysticisms which deny intellect altogether[8].

The skills of critical thinking are also needed by the Christian for the purpose of being able to answer his own questions about the Christian faith. As the Christian studies the Word of God, and through his interactions in the world, questions will arise about his faith, just as it did with Marty Sampson, and he will need to find an answer. The Christian will also need critical thinking skills to be able to answer the questions raised by the lost as he goes about the task of fulfilling the Great Commission.

There are Christians who will claim there is no need for training in critical thinking skills, reasoning that all you need is faith. But faith and critical thinking do go together. Thomas A. Howe and Richard G. Howe write:

> While it is the Holy Spirit who enables someone to believe, he may sometimes use the presentation of evidence for the Christian faith as the means whereby someone can come to

---

8 C. S. Lewis, "Learning in War Time," in *The Weight of Glory* (New York: HarperCollins Publishers, 1980), 58.

see the truth of the gospel. There is no conflict between the work of the Holy Spirit and the use of evidence and reason. The evidence and reason as such were never intended to supplant the work of God's Spirit but rather are intended to be the means by which the Holy Spirit brings someone to faith in Christ[9].

The goal of this book is to demonstrate the need for believers to develop and utilize critical thinking skills for the purpose of being able to respond to logical fallacies raised against the biblical worldview and to do so in a manner that may create an opportunity for sharing the gospel.

---

9 Thomas A. Howe and Richard G. Howe, "Knowing Christianity Is True: The Relationship Between Faith and Reason," in *To Everyone An Answer: A Case for the Christian Worldview* (Downers Grove: IVP Academic, 2004), 32–3.

Chapter 2

BIBLICAL FOUNDATIONS FOR CRITICAL THINKING

—————

Christians need to develop critical thinking skills to be better equipped to defend their faith and talk logically, reasonably, and rationally about the truth of the gospel. Joel McDurmon states that man's thinking ability depends upon the God of the Bible. He writes, "God both creates the human mind and determines the laws and conditions that govern man's thinking. Thus, God makes logical reasoning possible, meaningful, and reliable."[10] Jerram Barrs writes, "A fundamental part of our calling is to demolish arguments and every pretension that sets itself up against the true knowledge of God, and to take captive every thought to make it obedient to Christ."[11]

The foundation for the development of critical thinking

—————

10   Joel McDurmon, *Biblical Logic In Theory & Practice* (Powder Springs: American Vision Press, 2011), 31.
11   Jerram Barrs, "The Christian Mind," *L'Abri Papers* #JB03, accessed September 8, 2020, https://www.yumpu.com/en/document/view/37610252/the-christian-mind-jerram-barrs-labri-fellowship.

skills is the Word of God. In Colossians 2:8, the Apostle Paul writes, "See to it that no one takes you captive through philosophy and empty deception, according to the tradition of men, according to the elementary principles of the world, rather than according to Christ." According to Ian McNaughton, the Colossian believers were "...in danger of being deceived by human wisdom that is based on an unbiblical worldview."[12] McNaughton points out that this human wisdom included "... philosophy, traditions of men, science of the day, and worldly thinking."[13] In describing the "philosophy" being referred to, Arthur Patzia writes:

> This is the only time that the word *philosophia* occurs in the New Testament, so it must have been a special feature of this heresy. Paul is not objecting to the study of philosophy (lit., "one who loves wisdom"), because in the Hellenistic world religious communities offered their teaching as philosophy. His concern is with those who have turned the pursuit of wisdom into a "philosophistry" characterized by empty and deceitful practices. This teaching is hollow because it does not contain truth; it is deceptive because it captivates people and prevents them from seeing the truth[14].

---

12 Ian S. McNaughton, *Opening Up Colossians and Philemon*, Opening Up Commentary (Leominster: Day One Publications, 2006), 42.
13 McNaughton, Opening Up, 42.
14 Arthur G. Patzia, *Ephesians, Colossians, Philemon, New International Biblical Commentary*, vol. 10 (Peabody: Hendrickson Publishers, 1990), 51.

F. F. Bruce states:

> ...this philosophy was but empty illusion. If the Colossians embraced it, they would be the losers and not the gainers thereby. Those who knew what they were about when they "received Christ Jesus as Lord" could not find it acceptable; it was a human tradition which overthrew the essential truths of Christian faith and life.[15]

Warren Wiersbe describes those who are taken captive as being "...ignorant of the truths of the Word of God.[16]" The Colossians were being warned to keep their guard up, to be on the alert for the trickery, the cunning craftiness, and the deceitful plotting of these false teachers who were attempting to lead them away from the truth of the Christian faith.

If the Christian is to avoid being taken captive by the philosophy of an unbiblical worldview, he must prepare himself through the study of the Bible, God's word of truth. The Apostle Paul writes in 2 Timothy 2:15, "Be diligent to present yourself approved to God as a workman who does not need to be ashamed, accurately handling the word of truth." The antidote to the philosophy of an unbiblical worldview is a correct un-

---

15 F. F. Bruce, *The Epistles to the Colossians to Philemon and to Ephesians, The New International Commentary on the New Testament* (Grand Rapids: William B. Eerdmans Publishing Company, 1984), 98.
16 Warren W. Wiersbe, *The Bible Exposition Commentary*, vol. 2 (Wheaton: Victor Books, 1996), 125.

derstanding of the truths of the Christian faith.

Paul states that the Christian must "be diligent" in his handling of God's Word. The phrase "be diligent" comes from a Greek verb that means "to be eager, zealous, to have an intense desire."[17] It is in the imperative mood, which means it is a command for the believer. The phrase "accurately handling" comes from a Greek verb meaning "to give accurate instruction, to teach correctly, to expound rightly.[18]" According to Knofel Staton, "It literally means to cut straight. Don't be taking side detours with the Word. Don't be cutting corners. Don't be dodging the important issues[19]." William Mounce adds emphasis to the meaning of "accurately handling" in describing the adjective form of the Greek word from which it is derived. He writes:

> The adjective ὀρθός can also mean "straight, correct" (BAGD, 580), and according to Klober was used in secular Greek for "ethically correct behavior" and in the wisdom literature for "the kind of right attitude, speech, and action that accords with a proper relationship to Yahweh. It does

17 H.G. Liddell, A Lexicon: *Abridged from Liddell and Scott's Greek-English Lexicon* (Oak Harbor: Logos Research Systems, Inc., 1996), 741.
18 Johannes P. Louw and Eugene Albert Nida, *Greek-English Lexicon of the New Testament: Based on Semantic Domains* (New York: United Bible Societies, 1996), 414.
19 Knofel Staton, *Timothy-Philemon* (Cincinnati: Standard Publishing, 1988), 142.

not describe a virtue as much as a relationship" (NIDNTT 3:351)[20].

The main idea is that the Christian must have an intense desire, developed from an intimate relationship with God, to proclaim and expound the truth of the Scriptures. This desire, coupled with critical thinking skills, will assist the believer in confronting logical fallacies raised against the biblical worldview.

Two passages that help in understanding the connection between the development of critical thinking skills and the love a believer has for God are Deuteronomy 6:5 and Matthew 22:37.

Deuteronomy 6:5, "You shall love the Lord your God with all your heart and with all your soul and with all your might."

Matthew 22:37, "And He said to him, 'You shall love the Lord your God with all your heart, and with all your soul, and with all your mind.'"

In Deuteronomy 6:5, "heart" in Old Testament physiology "...refers to the mind or will, the center of the intellect."[21] Christopher Wright says it is "...the seat of the intellect, will,

20 William D. Mounce, *Pastoral Epistles, Word Biblical Commentary*, vol. 46 (Grand Rapids: Zondervan, 2000), 525.
21 Eugene H. Merrill, *Deuteronomy, Cornerstone Biblical Commentary: Leviticus, Numbers, Deuteronomy, ed. Philip W. Comfor*t, vol. 2 (Carol Stream: Tyndale House Publishers, 1996), 516.

and intention. You think in your heart, and your heart shapes your character, choices, and decisions."[22] Wright also explains that to love God "…with all your heart and with all your soul, means with your whole self, including your rationality, mental capacity, moral choices and will, inner feelings and desires, and the deepest roots of your life.[23]" Critical thinking skills are what will aid the believer in making rational decisions and moral choices that will challenge the fallacious arguments raised against the biblical worldview. Commenting on this verse, Ambrose, the bishop of Milan (374–397 AD), writes, "It is ever more seemly that you should give to God the most precious thing you have, that is, your mind.[24]"

In Matthew 22:37, Jesus was asked by an expert in the Mosaic Law, which is the greatest commandment. He answered by quoting Deuteronomy 6:5, but with one change: Jesus substituted the word "mind" for "might." Craig Bloomberg explains that the change in words does not affect the meaning of the mandate because "Both refer to wholehearted devotion to God with every aspect of one's being, from whatever angle one chooses to consider it—emotionally, volitionally, or

22 Christopher Wright, *Deuteronomy, New International Biblical Commentary,* vol. 4 (Peabody: Hendrickson Publishers, 2000), 99.
23 Christopher Wright, *Deuteronomy, Understanding the Bible Commentary Series* (Grand Rapids: Baker Books, 1996), 99.
24 *On the Duties of the Clergy,* New Advent, accessed December 7, 2019, https://www.newadvent.org/fathers/3401.htm.

cognitively.[25]" R. T. France writes, "*Dianoia* ('mind') perhaps indicates more our intellectual commitment."[26] In answering as He did, Jesus was informing the legal expert that the greatest commandment is to love God with all your being, and that would include the rational and logical thinking process.

It is interesting that the question raised by the legal expert followed an attempt by the Sadducees to trap Jesus through a scenario based around the law of the levirate marriage[27]. According to Deuteronomy 25:5–6, "…a brother is responsible for marrying a deceased brother's widow who has had no offspring in order to try to perpetuate the family line."[28] The purpose of their question was to make Jesus look foolish in front of His followers. In their scenario, a woman had successively been married to seven brothers; all had died without leaving any children. Their question was: In the resurrection, which husband would have her since they had all been married to her?

Jesus was not fooled by their question, nor did it stump Him; instead, using critical thinking skills, He demonstrated

25 Craig Blomberg, *Matthew, The New American Commentary*, vol. 22 (Nashville: Broadman & Holman Publishers, 1992), 335.

26 R. T. France, *Matthew: An Introduction and Commentary*, Tyndale New Testament Commentaries, vol. 1 (Downers Grove: InterVarsity Press, 1985), 323.

27 Barney Kasdan, *Matthew Presents Yeshua, King Messiah: A Messianic Commentary* (Clarksville: Messianic Jewish Publishers, 2011), 253.

28 *Blomberg*, Matthew, 333.

the weakness in their challenge. In commenting on this encounter, J. P. Moreland writes:

> Two things are important about the narrative. First, Jesus revealed His intellectual skills in debate by: (1) showing His familiarity with His opponents point of view; (2) appealing to common ground (a text all disputants accepted) instead of expressing a biblical text accepted but they rejected (Daniel 12:2); and (3) deftly using the laws of logic to dissect His opponents' argument and refute it powerfully. Second, because it forms the immediately preceding context for Matthew 22:37–39, this incident may inform at least part of what it means to love God intellectually: to be prepared to stand up for God's truth and honor when they are challenged to do so with carefully thought-out answers.[29]

In their challenge to Jesus, the Sadducees were unknowingly using a logical fallacy known today as a "false dilemma." This fallacy occurs "…when someone attempts to force a choice between two options even though other options exist.[30]" The Sadducees were trying to show that there were only two options for Jesus, either the woman would belong to one of the seven husbands, since they all could not have her, or there would be no resurrection. The third option, which Jesus

---

29 J. P. Moreland, *Loving God With All Your Mind* (Colorado Springs: NavPress, 2012), 53–4.

30 McDurmon, *Biblical Logic*, 103.

pointed out, is that they have misunderstood the Scriptures, which He then explained. The goal of this book is to show Christians how to employ critical thinking skills to refute fallacious arguments by pointing to other scripture, as did Jesus.

In Romans 12:1–2, the Apostle Paul issues the following command to the Christian:

> Therefore I urge you, brethren, by the mercies of God, to present your bodies a living and holy sacrifice, acceptable to God, which is your spiritual service of worship. And do not be conformed to this world, but be transformed by the renewing of your mind, so that you may prove what the will of God is, that which is good and acceptable and perfect.

In describing the phrase "spiritual service of worship," Robert Mounce writes, "This expression has been variously translated as 'spiritual service, reasonable worship, rational service,' and so on. Perhaps the best paraphrase is that of Knox, 'This is the worship due from you as rational creatures.'"[31] According to Charles Hodge, "The word translated here as 'spiritual' is explained in various ways. The simplest explanation is that which takes the word in its natural sense, 'pertaining to the mind.' It is a mental or spiritual service in opposition to cere-

---

31 Robert H. Mounce, *Romans, The New American Commentary*, vol. 27 (Nashville: Broadman & Holman Publishers, 1995), 231–32.

monial or external observances."[32]

The method by which this rational or mental service is accomplished is through the renewing of the mind. Grant Osborne explains why this is important: "The forces of 'this age' are invading and gaining control, forcing believers and unbelievers alike to conform to its ideals—consumerism, the desire for status and success, the pleasure principle, sex and good looks, and so on."[33] James Edwards agrees, "Modern society beams a collage of intense images at believers and non-believers alike through the media, advertising, polls, style, social and materialistic pressure, and ideologies. These images are often most effective when they are least recognized."[34] The mind must be renewed through the study of God's Word so that these images, whether they come in the form of fallacious arguments raised against the biblical worldview or societal pressures, can be recognized. According to Osborne, this renewal is "…a lifelong process in which our thinking is rescued from the influence of the world and reprogrammed to 'have in mind the concerns of God.'"[35] The word "mind," according to

---

32 Charles Hodge, *Romans, The Crossway Classic Commentaries* (Wheaton: Good News Publishers, 1993), 344.

33 Grant R. Osborne, *Romans: Verse by Verse, Osborne New Testament Commentaries* (Bellingham: Lexham Press, 2017), 381.

34 James R. Edwards, *Romans, New International Biblical Commentary,* vol. 6 (Peabody: Hendrickson Publishers, 1992), 284.

35 James R. Edwards, *Romans, New International Biblical Commentary,* vol. 6 (Peabody: Hendrickson Publishers, 1992), 284.

David Emanuel, "…appears in the New Testament mainly in the letters of Paul. It is a key term for describing the faculty of thinking, thought processing, and understanding."[36] Those faculties are part of critical thinking skills.

According to Barrs:

We are living in a culture which largely dismisses Christianity as irrelevant and irrational. Christianity is considered by many in our society to be the refuge of the weak who can't cope with the problems of life—they believe that you have to commit intellectual suicide if you are going to become a Christian.[37]

Barr goes on to say, "The world in its rebellion against God thinks that the gospel is foolish in contrast to its own ideas and philosophy. The world, the society in which we live, thinks that its own ideas are wisdom and that the gospel is folly."[38]

The challenges raised by the unbelieving world are ever-increasing and changing; therefore, the Christian must continually strive to develop his critical thinking skills. The Apostle Peter reinforces this belief in 1 Peter 3:15; he writes, "But

---

36 David M. Emanuel, "Thinking," in *Lexham Theological Wordbook*, *Lexham Bible Reference Series*, ed. Douglas Mangum et al. (Bellingham: Lexham Press, 2014).

37 Barrs, "The Christian Mind," 2.

38 Barrs, "The Christian Mind," 6.

sanctify Christ as Lord in your hearts, always being ready to make a defense to everyone who asks you to give an account for the hope that is in you, yet with gentleness and reverence." Peter has issued a mandate for the Christian to always be prepared to give an answer as to why he has placed his hope and faith in the gospel. Thomas Schreiner explains:

> The exhortation here is instructive, for Peter assumed that believers have solid intellectual grounds for believing the gospel. The truth of the gospel is a public truth that can be defended in the public arena. This does not mean, of course, that every Christian is to be a highly skilled apologist for the faith. It does mean that every believer should grasp the essentials of the faith and should have the ability to explain to others why they think the Christian faith is true.[39]

Peter begins his exhortation with the command for the believers to "sanctify Christ as Lord in your hearts." Peter Davids states, "The point of the text is clear. The heart is the seat of volition and emotion for Peter, the core self of the person. The call is for more than an intellectual commitment to truth about Jesus, but for a deep commitment to Him."[40] That deep

---

39 Thomas R. Schreiner, *1, 2, Peter, Jude The New American Commentary*, vol. 37 (Nashville: Broadman & Holman Publishers, 2003), 174–75.
40 Peter H. Davids, *The First Epistle of Peter, The New International Commentary on the New Testament* (Grand Rapids: William B. Eerdmans Publishing Company, 1990), 131.

commitment and love for God will motivate the believer to always be prepared to give an answer for the hope he has in Him.

There are two key words that are central to the meaning of Peter's statement: "defense" and "account." The word "defense" comes from the Greek word *apologia* and means "to speak on behalf of oneself or of others against accusations presumed to be false."[41] According to Kenneth Wuest, *apologia* "…was used of an attorney who talked his client off from a charge preferred against him. He presented a verbal defense. The exhortation is to Christians to talk the Bible off from the charges preferred against it, thus presenting for it a verbal defense."[42] The word "account" comes from the Greek word *logos*, and in the context of 1 Peter 3:15, means, "a reason, with the implication of some verbal formulation."[43] J. P. Moreland defines it as "…evidence or argument which provides rational justification for some belief."[44] Moreland goes on to say, "Peter is saying that we are to be prepared to give rational arguments and good reasons for why we believe, and this involves the mind.[45]" Charles Spurgeon would agree, for he writes:

41 Louw and Nida, *Greek-English Lexicon*, 437.
42 Kenneth S. Wuest, *Wuest's Word Studies from the Greek New Testament: For the English Reader*, vol. 11 (Grand Rapids: Eerdmans, 1997), 89.
43 Louw and Nida, *Greek-English Lexicon*, 778.
44 Moreland, *Loving God*, 54.
45 Moreland, *Loving God*, 55.

We want Bible students as Christians—men who not only believe the truth but have good reasons for believing it. We want men who can meet error with the argument, "It is written," and can maintain the truth at all hazards, using weapons taken from the armory of God's inspired Book. Oh, that we had among us more who were fit to be teachers! May we grow in grace so that, when the question is asked, "Who is this?" we may be able to answer it. Covet earnestly this spiritual gift of knowledge, and give yourselves diligently to the search after it, that you may become fully established in the principles of the gospel of Jesus Christ. What a blessing you will be to others if you have much knowledge of the things of God![46]

It is also important to understand that critical thinking skills, according to Peter Kreeft, come from God. They are a gift, but He does not do our critical thinking for us[47]. He provides two reasons why he considers critical thinking skills a gift, yet the believer is responsible for developing them:

First, because it is the exercise of an essential part of the image of God in us. God does not think our thoughts for us, yet our minds are dependent on God's mind just as totally as the existence of the physical universe is dependent on God's

46 Charles Spurgeon, *Spurgeon Commentary: 1 Peter, Spurgeon Commentary Series*, eds. Elliot Ritzema and Jessi Strong (Bellingham: Lexham Press, 2014), 1 Peter 3:15.
47 Kreeft, "Critical Thinking," 5.

will to "let it be" and on God's power to do all that He wills. Our minds are mirrors, and God is the sun, and all the light we generate is reflected light from Him; yet it is our choice to turn our mirrors to the sun or not, and to keep them clean or not, and to keep them unbroken or to break them into fragments. Every time we think wrongly, we misuse a divine gift, just as whenever we misuse our free will we misuse a divine gift. Both wrong thinking and wrong choosing are sacrileges, because they desecrate a holy thing. What we pervert in wrong thinking is the mirrored powers of God's own mind that He gave us in giving us His own image. We pervert this image whenever we move our minds into the dark and away from the light, just as we pervert the mirrored powers of God's will which He gave us in giving us free will as part of His image in us, whenever we move our wills to evil and away from good. God continues to uphold in existence His spiritual gifts, the two powers of His image in us, even when we pervert them, just as He continues to uphold the physical universe even when we misuse it. The second reason critical thinking is God's gift is because grace perfects nature, and this is an essential part of human nature, the ability and the desire to think logically as a means to thinking truly.[48]

McDurmon agrees that critical thinking is a gift from God. He writes, "Man's thinking depends upon the God of the Bi-

---

48 Kreeft, "*Critical Thinking*," 5.

ble. It depends upon Him for its being and order: God both creates the human mind and determines the laws and conditions that govern man's thinking. Thus, God makes logical reasoning possible, meaningful, and reliable.[49]" For that reason, the Christian should strive to develop this gift.

Christians need critical thinking skills to evaluate all charges and arguments raised against the biblical worldview in an attempt to discover their veracity or falsity. Paul exhorts the Thessalonian believers to do just that in 1 Thessalonians 5:21–22, "But examine everything carefully; hold fast to that which is good; abstain from every form of evil."

Paul's use of the verb "examine," according to Juan Valdes, "...is synonymous with critical thinking[50]." It is translated from the Greek word *dokimazō*, which "...has the notion of proving a thing whether it is worthy or not."[51] Valdes states, "While the context of this exhortation pertains to prophecy, the terminology and the principles involved can be applied to critical thinking in general. Critical thinking is about testing all things (ideas)."[52]

---

49 McDurmon, Biblical Logic, 31.
50 Juan Valdes, "A Biblical Foundation for Critical Thinking," *Reasons for Hope*, accessed March 6, 2020, https://www.rforh.com/blog/2015/09/30/a-biblical-foundation-for-critical-thinking.
51 Spiros Zodhiates, *The Complete Word Study Dictionary: New Testament* (Chattanooga: AMG Publishers, 1992), 1381.
52 Valdes, "Biblical Foundation," 2.

In his exhortation to the believers at Thessalonica, Paul includes some very practical applications for critical thinking, which are pertinent to believers today. Valdes explains:

> First, every idea should be subjected to critical analysis (testing). Second, critical thinking helps distinguish between good and evil. In other words, it helps us identify those ideas that are biblical (good) and those that are contrary to what is taught in the Bible (evil). Third, critical thinking is of utmost important when deciding how to live our lives. We are to "hold fast to what is good" and we are to "abstain from every form of evil."[53]

Paul shunned worldly wisdom and instead advocated the standard of God's wisdom. He called Christians in light of this standard to examine all things critically.

First Corinthians 2:6–7:

> Yet we do speak wisdom among those who are mature; a wisdom, however, not of this age nor of the rulers of this age, who are passing away; But we speak God's wisdom in a mystery, the hidden wisdom which God predestined before the ages to our glory.

---

53 Valdes, "Biblical Foundation," 2.

First Corinthians 2:12–15:

Now we have received, not the spirit of the world, but the spirit who is from God, so that we may know the things freely given to us by God, which things we also speak, not in words taught by human wisdom, but in those taught by the spirit, combining spiritual thoughts with spiritual words. But a natural man does not accept the things of the spirit of God, for they are foolishness to him; and he cannot understand them, because they are spiritually appraised. But he who is spiritual appraises all things, yet he himself is appraised by no one.

The connection to critical thinking is made by the phrase "spiritually appraised." The verb "appraised" comes from the Greek word *anakrino* and means "to make a judgment on the basis of careful and detailed information; to judge carefully, to evaluate carefully."[54] A. T. Robertson states, "The word means a sifting process to get at the truth by investigation as of a judge."[55] Robert Utley defines it as "…a legal term that speaks of the preliminary exhaustive examination before a trial."[56] The root word for *anakrino* is *krino*, and it has the meaning of

---

54 Louw and Nida, *Greek-English Lexicon*, 363.
55 A. T. Robertson, *Word Pictures in the New Testament* (Nashville: Broadman Press, 1933), 1 Corinthians 2:14.
56 Robert James Utley, *Paul's Letters to a Troubled Church: I and II Corinthians, Study Guide Commentary Series*, vol. 6 (Marshall: Bible Lessons International, 2002), 38.

"to come to a conclusion in the process of thinking and thus to be in a position to make a decision."[57] This is critical thinking and should be practiced by every individual who is filled with God's Holy Spirit. Gordon Fee states it well, "Paul allows that the truly 'spiritual' person, the one who understands what God has done in Christ crucified, discerns, 'examines' all things.[58]"

According to McDurmon:

> Jesus, the embodiment and exemplar of faithful human thinking, engaged in faithful critical thinking (judgment) in obedience to the will of the Father: "As I hear, I judge (*krino*); and My judgment (*krisis*) is just, because I do not seek My own will, but the will of Him who sent Me (John 5:30)." We should not avoid critical thinking, but rather, like Jesus, engage in faithful critical thinking in submission to our Father in Heaven[59].

Isaiah 1:18 supports this proposition, "'Come now, and let us reason together,' Says the Lord, 'Though your sins are as scarlet, They will be as white as snow; Though they are red like crimson, They will be like wool.'" The verb "reason" comes from the Hebrew word *yākaḥ*. John Martin states that it "…is

---

57 Louw and Nida, *Greek-English Lexicon*, 358.
58 Gordon Fee, T*he First Epistle to the Corinthians, The New International Commentary on the New Testamen*t (Grand Rapids: William B. Eerdmans Publishing Company, 1987), 118.
59 McDurmon, *Biblical Logic*, 54.

a law term used of arguing, convincing, or deciding a case in court. The people were to be convinced by their argumentation with God that He was right and they were wrong about their condition.[60]" McDurmon explains that the "English translation 'reason' today carries overtones of individual scholarship or thinking, and these lead us away from Isaiah's context of God's lawsuit against Israel for breaking the laws of His covenant."[61] He further writes:

> God called Israel to a debate that required critical thinking with His word as the standard. Rebellious Israel would have been wise to accept His gracious terms, for they could not have reasoned successfully against God's covenant terms. He issued the challenge in order to jerk their thinking to reality, saying in effect, "Let us dispute," in order to know "if I do accuse you without cause."[62]

In summation, McDurmon asserts:

> Rather than fear critical thinking, Christians should seek to reclaim, reform, and embrace it. We must exercise "judgment" in conforming our lives to God's Word; we should seek to expand the area of that influence further into our

---

60 John A. Martin, *Isaiah, The Bible Knowledge Commentary: An Exposition of the Scriptures*, vol. 1, eds. J. F. Walvoord and R. B. Zuck (Wheaton: Victor Books, 1985), 1036.
61 McDurmon, *Biblical Logic*, 57.
62 McDurmon, *Biblical Logic*, 57.

lives, and should embrace the idea of learning to "judge." This follows a scriptural ideal. The apostles, Jesus promised, would sit upon thrones in judgment over Israel (Matthew 19:28; Luke 22:30). Paul argued that all Christians will sit in judgment over the world and even angels (1 Corinthians 6:2–3), and should therefore have the critical thinking skills to arbitrate each others' minor disputes (1 Corinthians 6:4–6). Moses reminded the Israelites that he taught them God's law, and thus standards for good judgment: "I have taught you statutes and judgments just as the Lord my God commanded me, that you should do thus in the land where you are entering to possess it" (Deuteronomy 4:5, 14). We should employ godly logic and reasoning, and recapture business, ethics, law, education, and everything else, "destroying speculations and every lofty thing raised up against the knowledge of God, and we are taking every thought captive to the obedience of Christ" (2 Corinthians 10:5).[63]

McDurmon uses 2 Corinthians 10:5 to support his claim that Christians need not fear critical thinking but develop it, "We are destroying speculations and every lofty thing raised up against the knowledge of God, and we are taking every thought captive to the obedience of Christ." In this passage, George Guthrie believes, "Paul says the powerful weapons of ministry warfare dismantle 'argument,' walls of wrong thinking that

---

63 McDurmon, *Biblical Logic*, 58.

stand in opposition to right Christian teaching.[64]" He explains that the participle "destroying" has two objects. "The first, logismous, refers to 'thoughts,' calculations,' 'reasonings,' or 'reflections,' thus 'argument' in our translations."[65] The second object of the participle is the phrase, "We are destroying speculations and every lofty thing raised up against the knowledge of God, and we are taking every thought captive to the obedience of Christ." Guthrie explains that the "thoughts" refer to "…an enemy wall standing against a true knowledge of God; authentic Christian ministry tears down such thoughts and makes clear the gospel.[66]" This is what the skills of critical thinking will enable the believer to accomplish.

The continual development of critical thinking skills is a must for the believer and will be a great aid to him in being able to explain why the gospel is true and worthy of his faith and hope. As Paul Gould states, "Justified true beliefs will help us live and help us love, because we love best what we know best.[67]" We will love God best when we know Him best!

64 George H. Guthrie, *2 Corinthians, Baker Exegetical Commentary on the New Testament* (Grand Rapids: Baker Academic, 2015), 474.

65 Guthrie, *2 Corinthians*, 474–75.

66 Guthrie, *2 Corinthians*, 475

67 Paul M. Gould, *Cultural Apologetics: Renewing the Christian Voice, Conscience, and Imagination in a Disenchanted World* (Grand Rapids: Zondervan, 2019), 128.

Chapter 3

CRITICAL THINKING AND EVANGELISM

———

Engaging in evangelism is where the Christian will discover the need for critical thinking skills. Often, he will encounter an unbeliever who needs help in overcoming obstacles to Christianity before his heart will be open to hearing the message of salvation. Those obstacles could be issues such as the problem of evil, the conflict between science and the Bible, and the Christian position on many of the social issues (abortion, homosexuality, same-sex marriage, transgenderism) within our culture today.

Critical thinking skills can help the believer identify the obstacle and respond in a way that may open the heart of the unbeliever to hear and respond to the voice of the Holy Spirit. Randy Newman explains:

> Proclaiming the gospel is powerful. We trust in the Holy Spirit, who "will prove the world to be in the wrong about sin and righteousness and judgment" (John 16:8) as we do

so. But we must notice that the Scriptures offer a variety of preparations for the gospel before stating the message outright[68].

Newman calls these preparations, of which critical thinking skills would play a role, "pre-evangelism."[69] He is convinced that "…pre-evangelism is essential for reaching people with the gospel in postmodern settings today."[70]

Francis Schaeffer stated that "Pre-evangelism is not a soft option."[71] He shared the following experience:

Some time ago I was speaking at Oxford University to a group of theological students on the subject of communicating the gospel to those people who are dominated by the consensus of twentieth-century thinking. When I had finished speaking, a Canadian post-graduate student stood up and said, "Sir, if we understand you correctly, you are saying that pre-evangelism must come before evangelism.

68 Randy Newman, *Unlikely Converts: Improbable Stories of Faith and What They Teach Us About Evangelism* (Grand Rapids: Kregel Publications, 2019), 21.
69 "Evangelism" is the verbal proclamation of a very specific message; that Jesus died to atone for sins, that he rose from the dead, and that people must respond with repentance and faith. "Pre-evangelism" refers to the many different things that can pave the way for that proclamation. (Newman, *Unlikely Converts,* 21.)
70 Newman, *Unlikely Converts*, 20.
71 Francis Schaeffer, *The God Who Is There* (Downers Grove: IVP Books, 1982), 169.

If this is so, then we have been making a mistake at Oxford. The reason we have not been reaching many of these people is because we have not taken enough time with pre-evangelism." I said that I totally agreed.[72]

In a YouTube video titled "Pre-Evangelism,"[73] R. C. Sproul discusses the role of pre-evangelism in leading a person to a saving faith in Jesus Christ. He presents three levels or elements of faith that together comprise saving faith: *notitia, assensus,* and *fiducia.* The words themselves are simply common Latin words. Timothy Jones defines them as follows:

In *notitia* the individual becomes aware of the conditions, promises, and events that constitute divine revelation, especially the events surrounding God's consummate self-revelation in Jesus Christ. In assensus the individual expresses objective confidence in the truthfulness of these claims (Romans 10:9; Hebrews 11:3, 6; 1 John 5:1). In fiducia the individual places his or her personal trust in Jesus Christ.[74]

J. P. Moreland and Klaus Issler add support to Jones's definitions of the terms. They write:

---

72 Schaeffer, *The God,* 175.
73 R. C. Sproul, "Pre-Evangelism," YouTube video, 23:47, accessed August 15, 2020, https://www.youtube.com/watch?v=_3o1UAnsL74.
74 Timothy Paul Jones, "The Necessity of Objective Assent in the Act of Christian Faith," *Bibliotheca Sacra* 162 (April-June 2005), 150.

Notitia refers to the content of faith, primarily the assertions of Scripture and theological, doctrinal formulations derived from Scripture. Thus, Jude 3 says, "I felt I had to write and urge you to contend for *the faith* that was once for all entrusted to the saints" (emphasis added). Learning to think theologically, to develop a biblical worldview, to grasp and understand the teachings of Christianity is essential to a vibrant faith. *Notitia* is also defined as knowledge of the meaning of or as understanding the content of doctrinal teaching. This clearly implies that far from being antithetical to faith, knowledge is actually an important ingredient of it.[75]

Assensus refers to personal assent to, awareness of or agreement with the truth of Christian teaching, and, again, it is primarily intellectual, though there are clear affective and psychological components to *assensus*. Medieval theologians distinguished varying degrees of assent to something, with "full assent without hesitation" as the strongest form. The important thing is that it is not enough to *grasp* the contents of Christian teaching; one must also accept the fact that this teaching is true.[76]

Fiducia involves personal commitment to its object, whether to a truth or a person. *Fiducia* is essentially a matter of the

---

75 J. P. Moreland and Klaus Issler, *In Search of a Confident Faith: Overcoming Barriers to Trusting in God* (Downers Grove: 2008), chap. 1, page 19, Kindle.
76 Moreland and Issler, *In Search*, chap. 1, page 20, Kindle.

will, but because Christianity is a relationship with a Person and not just commitment to a set of truths (though this is, of course, essential), the capacity to develop emotional intimacy and to discern the inner movements of feeling, intuition and God's Spirit in the soul is crucial to maintaining and cultivating commitment to God.[77]

Moreland and Craig explain how the three levels work together to bring someone to saving faith:

Trust is based on understanding, knowledge and the intellect's assent to truth. Belief in rests on belief *that*. One is called to trust in what he or she has reason to give intellectual assent (*assensus*) to. In Scripture, faith involves placing trust in what you have reason to believe is true. Faith is not a blind, irrational leap into the dark. So faith and reason cooperate on a biblical view of faith.[78]

It is through the use of the skills of critical thinking that a Christian can identify the obstacle to the gospel and then, based on Scripture, provide an understanding of the Christian view of that obstacle. This provides the unbeliever with the information needed to allow him to give intellectual assent to the truth of the proposition of the gospel (pre-evangelism).

---

77 Moreland and Issler, *In Search*, chap. 1, page 21, Kindle.
78 J. P. Moreland and William Lane Craig, *Philosophical Foundations For A Christian Worldview* (Downers Grove: IVP Academic, 2003), 18.

Now the individual is possibly open to hearing the convicting voice of the Holy Spirit "...concerning sin, righteousness, and judgment" (John 16:8).

An example of the process of these elements, pre-evangelism, in saving faith can be found in 1 Thessalonians 2:13:

> For this reason we also constantly thank God that when you received the word of God [i.e., *notitia*, information about Jesus] which you heard from us, you accepted it not as the word of men [i.e., *assensus*, intellectually assenting to the truth of the proposition being made is, in fact, the very words of God], but for what it really is, the word of God, which also performs its work in you who believe [i.e., *fiducia*, placing trust in that word, the gospel of Jesus Christ, leading to saving faith].[79]

The verbal phrase "when you received" comes from the Greek verb *paralambano* and conveys the idea of "receiving information or receiving of someone or something into a subject's jurisdiction or care."[80] According to Leon Morris, the word

---

79 "What is the background of the words 'notitia,' 'fiducia,' and 'assensus' and how do they relate to the biblical notion of 'faith'?" Christianity Stack Exchange, accessed September 5, 2020, https://christianity.stackexchange.com/questions/31589/what-is-the-background-of-the-words-notitia-fiducia-and-assensus-and-how.

80 Derek Leigh Davis, "Learning," in ed. Douglas Mangum et al., Lexham Theological Wordbook, *Lexham Bible Reference Series* (Bellingham: Lexham Press, 2014).

"...is one which denotes an objective, outward receiving."[81] David Ewert adds that paralambano was "...used regularly for receiving a body of instruction."[82] This would be the element of *notitia* in saving faith.

The verbal phrase "you accepted" comes from the Greek verb *dechomai* and means "to readily receive information and to regard it as true[83]." Morris states that it is a "...subjective reception, a reception which involves welcome and approval[84]." This would be the element of *assensus* in saving faith.

The task of pre-evangelism is complete, and now comes the convicting work of the Holy Spirit. This is not to say that the Holy Spirit has not been involved in the whole process, for He was at work in the *notitia* and *assensus*. Every opportunity to share the gospel is guided by the Holy Spirit. Acts 1:8 states, "But you will receive power when the Holy Spirit has come upon you; and you shall be My witnesses both in Jerusalem, and in all Judea and Samaria, and even to the remotest part of the earth." It is the Holy Spirit who empowers the believer to

---

81 Leon Morris, *The First and Second Epistles to the Thessalonians, The New International Commentary on the New Testament* (Grand Rapids: WM. B. Eerdmans Publishing, 1959), 88.

82 David Ewert, *1-2 Thessalonians, Evangelical Commentary on the Bible, Baker Reference Library,* vol. 3 (Grand Rapids: Baker Book House, 1995), 1074.

83 Louw and Nida, *Greek-English Lexicon,* 371.

84 Morris, *First and Second Epistles,* 88.

share the gospel, and it is He who gives him the words to speak as declared in Luke 12, "…for the Holy Spirit will teach you in that very hour what you ought to say." The verbal phrase "performs its work," in 1 Thessalonians 2:13, comes from the Greek verb *energeo* and means "to be in action or activity, operate."[85] According to Morris, this verb "…is almost always used in the New Testament of some form of supernatural activity. Mostly it is that of God. It can be used of such things as faith (Galatians 5:6), prayer (James 5:16), life or death (II Corinthians 4:12), in each case a force not human being involved."[86] The Thessalonians received the information about Christ and regarded it as true, resulting in the power of God, through the Holy Spirit, being released in their lives, bringing them into a saving faith, *fiducia*. As Knute Larson explains, "The power of God is released through faith in his Word; it becomes an active, spiritual energy, cutting like a scalpel to the depths of the soul (Heb. 4:12)."[87]

The Bible is a book filled with illustrations of the work of pre-evangelism. For example, Newman states that "The entire

---

85   Henry George Liddell et al., *A Greek Lexicon* (Oxford: Clarendon Press, 1996), 564.

86   Morris, *First and Second Epistles*, 88.

87   Knute Larson, *I & II Thessalonians, I & II Timothy, Titus, Philemon, Holman New Testament Commentary*, vol. 9 (Nashville: Broadman & Holman Publishers, 2000), 26.

Old Testament is pre-evangelistic."[88] In his view, "The Old Testament does far more to prepare our hearts for the Messiah than simply hint at his suffering; it moves us toward solving the mystery of who he will be."[89]

Genesis 22:13–14 is just one of those illustrations:

> Then Abraham raised his eyes and looked, and behold, behind him a ram caught in the thicket by his horns; and Abraham went and took the ram and offered him up for a burnt offering in the place of his son. Abraham called the name of that place The Lord Will Provide, as it is said to this day, "In the mount of the Lord it will be provided."

Newman explains that:

> Abraham offers up a son as a sacrifice but has the process halted by a God who provides his own substitute. The text itself lets us know this drama is not finished because it identifies the location as "The Lord Will Provide." You would have thought it should be called, "The Lord Did Provide." Apparently, this drama pointed to a future provision that will be better.[90]

The Hebrew verb from which the phrase "will provide" is de-

---

88 Newman, *Unlikely Converts*, 22.

89 Newman, *Unlikely Converts*, 23.

90 Newman, *Unlikely Converts*, 23.

rived is a prefixed conjugation, which "...views the action of the verb from the inside or from the perspective of the action's unfolding. This imperfective aspect can speak of (depending on context) habitual actions, actions in progress, or even completed actions that have unfolding, ongoing results."[91] So from the name "The Lord Will Provide," there is both *notitia*, information about a coming better sacrifice, and *assensus*, Abraham's belief in the truth of that proposition.

As for the New Testament, Newman writes, "The New Testament recounts instances of partial gospel proclamations. It gives us models and templates for pre-evangelism."[92] Peter's second sermon in Acts 3:11–26 is one example. Verses 12–16 contain Peter's truth claim—his argument:

> But when Peter saw this, he replied to the people, "Men of Israel, why are you amazed at this, or why do you gaze at us, as if by our own power or piety we had made him walk? The God of Abraham, Isaac and Jacob, the God of our fathers, has glorified His servant Jesus, the one whom you delivered and disowned in the presence of Pilate, when he had decided to release Him. But you disowned the Holy and Righteous One and asked for a murderer to be granted to you, but put to death the Prince of life, the one whom

---

91 Michael S. Heiser and Vincent M. Setterholm, *Glossary of Morpho-Syntactic Database Terminology* (Lexham Press, 2013).
92 Newman, *Unlikely Converts*, 24.

God raised from the dead, a fact to which we are witnesses. And on the basis of faith in His name, it is the name of Jesus which has strengthened this man whom you see and know; and the faith which comes through Him has given him this perfect health in the presence of you all."

Commenting on these verses, John Polhill writes:

Verses 12 and 16 go closely together. Verse 12 raises the question about the power behind the man's healing. Verse 16 provides the answer. In between is inserted the basic kerygma of the death and resurrection of Christ and the Jewish responsibility in those events. The basic function of vv. 13–15 is to establish the Jewish guilt in rejecting Jesus.[93]

The remainder of the sermon, verses 17–26, is basically an appeal to repent and affirm the truth about the identity of Jesus Christ. In verses 17–18:

Peter was offering the Jerusalem Jews a second chance. Once they had disowned the Christ. It was, however, a rejection in ignorance. Now they could accept Christ and be forgiven. Should they fail to do so once Peter gave them a full understanding of Christ's true identity, it would be a

---

93 John B. Polhill, *Acts, The New American Commentary*, vol. 26, (Nashville: Broadman & Holman Publishers, 1992), 130.

wholly different matter, a deliberate, "high-handed" rejection.[94]

(17-18) "And now, brethren, I know that you acted in ignorance, just as your rulers did also. But the things which God announced beforehand by the mouth of all the prophets, that His Christ would suffer, He has thus fulfilled."

Both the *notitia* and *assensus* levels of saving faith, pre-evangelism, are found in verses 17–26. The *fiducia* element occurs in Acts 4:4, "But many of those who had heard the message believed; and the number of the men came to be about five thousand." The verb "had heard" comes from a Greek word that means "to hear with 'understanding, comprehension.'"[95] The verb "believed" comes from a Greek word that is "…used in the New Testament of the conviction and trust to which a man is impelled by a certain inner and higher prerogative and law of soul.[96]" Louw and Nida state that it is "…to believe in the good news about Jesus Christ and to become a follower."[97]

The obstacle Peter had to overcome in his pre-evangelism

---

94 Polhill, *Acts*, 133.
95 Spiros Zodhiates, *The Complete Word Study Dictionary: New Testament* (Chattanooga, TN: AMG Publishers, 1992), 114.
96 James Strong, *Enhanced Strong's Lexicon* (Woodside Bible Fellowship, 1995).
97 Louw and Nida, *Greek-English Lexicon*, 378.

effort was the ignorance of the people as to who Jesus was. As F. F. Bruce states, "They did not realize that Jesus of Nazareth was their divinely sent Savior.[98]" Even after this effort, there were those who still refused to accept the truth of Peter's proposition. Only those who responded in faith to what Peter said would have experienced the life-transforming power of the Holy Spirit.

A second example from the New Testament is found in Paul's sermon on Mars Hill, Acts 17:22–34. The obstacle Paul faced here was the people were too religious. According to J. Vernon McGee, "The Athenians were very religious. Athens was filled with idols. There was no end to the pantheon of the Athenians and the Greeks. There were gods small and gods great; they had a god for practically everything. That is what Paul is saying. They were too religious.[99]" Stanley D. Toussaint adds, "The idea is that the Athenians were firm and rigid in their reverencing of their deities."[100] For this reason, Paul had to change his approach in preaching to the Athenians.

---

98 F. F. Bruce, *The Book of Acts, The New International Commentary on the New Testament* (Grand Rapids: William B. Eerdman's Publishing Company, 1988), 83.

99 J. Vernon McGee, *Thru the Bible Commentary: Church History* (Acts 15–28), electronic ed., vol. 41 (Nashville: Thomas Nelson, 1991), 51.

100 Stanley D. Toussaint, *Acts, The Bible Knowledge Commentary: An Exposition of the Scriptures, ed. J. F. Walvoord and R. B. Zuck,* vol. 2 (Wheaton: Victor Books, 1985), 403.

Bruce writes of Paul's approach:

> Here he does not quote Hebrew Scriptures which would have been quite unknown to his hearers; the direct quotations in this speech are quotations from Greek poets. But he does not condescend to his hearers' level by arguing from principles as one of their own philosophers might do. His argument is firmly based on biblical revelation; it echoes throughout the thought, and at times the very language, of the Old Testament. Like the biblical revelation itself, his argument begins with God the creator of all and ends with God the judge of all[101].

Paul formulated his approach to the Athenians with the gospel based upon their understanding of the spiritual world. Williams writes, "With the Areopagites a philosophical approach was demanded and an appeal not so much to the evidence of nature as to the inner witness of God to human consciousness and conscience.[102]" Paul's truth claim, proposition, is found in verses 22–25:

> So Paul stood in the midst of the Areopagus and said, "Men of Athens, I observe that you are very religious in all respects. For while I was passing through and examining the objects of your worship, I also found an altar with this in-

---

101   Bruce, *Book of Acts*, 335.
102   Williams, *1 and 2 Thessalonians*, 301.

scription, 'TO AN UNKNOWN GOD.' Therefore what you worship in ignorance, this I proclaim to you. The God who made the world and all things in it, since He is Lord of heaven and earth, does not dwell in temples made with hands; nor is He served by human hands, as though He needed anything, since He Himself gives to all people life and breath and all things."

The *notitia* is found in verses 26–31, and the *assensus* and *fiducia* in verses 32 and 34.

"And He made from one man every nation of mankind to live on all the face of the earth, having determined their appointed times and the boundaries of their habitation, that they would seek God, if perhaps they might grope for Him and find Him, though He is not far from each one of us; for in Him we live and move and exist, as even some of your own poets have said, 'For we also are His children.' Being then the children of God, we ought not to think that the Divine Nature is like gold or silver or stone, an image formed by the art and thought of man. Therefore having overlooked the times of ignorance, God is now declaring to men that all people everywhere should repent, because He has fixed a day in which He will judge the world in righteousness through a Man whom He has appointed, having furnished proof to all men by raising Him from the dead." Now when they heard of the resurrection of the dead, some began to sneer, but others said, "We shall hear you again concerning this." But some men joined him and believed, among whom also were Dionysius the Areopagite and a woman named Damaris and others with them.

Commenting on verse 32, Bruce writes:

The idea of resurrection of dead people was uncongenial to the minds of most of Paul's Athenian hearers. All of them except the Epicureans would no doubt have agreed with him had he spoken of the immortality of the individual soul; but as for resurrection, they would have endorsed the sentiments of the god Apollo, expressed on the occasion when that very court of the Areopagus was founded by the city's patron goddess Athene: "Once a man dies and the earth drinks up his blood, there is no resurrection." Some of them, therefore, ridiculed a statement which seemed so absurd. Others, more polite if equally skeptical, suggested that there might be an opportunity later for further exposition of his teaching.[103]

Polhill concurs with Bruce. He states:

Epicureans believed in no human existence after death. Stoics believed that only the immaterial spirit survived death. To Greeks the idea of a body surviving death did not make

103 Bruce, *Book of Acts*, 343.

any sense—even a transformed body. So many in the Areopagus simply scoffed at Paul's reference to the resurrection. As so often with the preaching of the gospel in Acts, however, the response was mixed. Others wanted to "hear [him] again." There is no reason to see this response as anything but genuine. They were not convinced by Paul, but they were still willing to give him further hearing.[104]

The Athenians had heard Paul's proposition and his supporting data, but some were not yet convinced of the truth of his evidence. They were willing, however, to hear him again. Sometimes in pre-evangelism, this happens because the evidence presented is not enough to overcome the obstacle. In this case, the obstacle for many was the resurrection. However, there were some who did join Paul, as indicated in verse 34. The verb "joined" comes from a Greek word meaning "to begin an association with someone, whether temporary or permanent; to join, to join oneself to, to become a part of."[105] They joined with Paul because they believed his proposition, his truth statement and placed their trust in Christ. The verb "believed" comes from a Greek word that "…expresses the idea of trust in or faithfulness to someone or something."[106]

---

104 Polhill, *Acts*, 378.
105 Louw and Nida, *Greek-English Lexicon*, 447.
106 Chris Kugler, "Faith," ed. Douglas Mangum et al., *Lexham Theological Wordbook, Lexham Bible Reference Series* (Bellingham: Lexham Press, 2014).

This was the *fiducia* element of saving faith for those who believed, two of which were named Dionysius and Damaris.

Pre-evangelism is an important part of the complete evangelism process. The goal of pre-evangelism is to provide the unbeliever with information about the content of our faith so that obstacles may be overcome, leading him possibly to conclude that the gospel is true, the *notitia* and *assensus* elements of saving faith.

Francis Schaeffer writes:

Before a man is ready to become a Christian, he must have a proper understanding of truth, whether he has fully analyzed his concept of truth or not. All people, whether they realize it or not, function in the framework of some concept of truth. Our concept of truth will radically affect our understanding of what it means to be a Christian. We are concerned at this point, not with the content of truth so much as with the concept of what truth is.[107]

It is here that Newman points out, "We must trust the Holy Spirit to open up blind eyes and soften hardened hearts. We realize the Holy Spirit must do the work of regeneration in order for our gospel proclamation to bear fruit."[108]

The Christian is going to face many challenges, obstacles

107 Schaeffer, *The God*, 175.
108 Newman, *Unlikely Converts*, 42.

to the biblical worldview because of sin and unbelief in the world. He must ask God to show him the obstacle behind each challenge the unbeliever raises against the Christian faith. As Newman explains, "People may ask questions with cool, unexpressive faces. But behind those faces, dramas play out that we can't even imagine. They may ask about evil and suffering because they've become ensnared in evil and suffering."[109] Training in the skills of critical thinking will help prepare the Christian to ask the right questions, to develop an effective pre-evangelism approach that will demonstrate to the unbeliever the truthfulness of the gospel, priming him for the work of the Holy Spirit in bringing him to a saving faith.

---

109 Newman, *Unlikely Converts,* 172.

Chapter 4

WHAT ARE LOGICAL FALLACIES?

———

As the Christian involves himself in fulfilling the Acts 1:8 mandate, he will encounter a culture that will offer arguments against his belief in the God of the Bible, and he must be prepared to respond, as Peter states in 1 Peter 3:15, "…with gentleness and reverence." "Gentleness" comes from the Greek noun *prautēs* and means "gentleness of attitude and behavior, in contrast with harshness in one's dealings with others.[110]" "Reverence" comes from the Greek noun *phobos* and, in the context of this verse, carries the idea of "…a feeling of profound respect for someone or something."[111] Schreiner explains:

> When believers encounter a hostile world and are challenged concerning their faith, the temptation to respond harshly increases. Defending a position could easily be transmuted

---

110 Louw and Nida, *Greek-English Lexicon*, 748.
111 *The Lexham Lexicon of the Greek New Testament* (Bellingham: Lexham Press, 2020).

into attacking one's opponents. Hence, Peter added that the defense must be made "with gentleness and reverence."[112]

As explained by William Hughes, Jonathan Lavery, and Kathryn Doran, "An argument is a set of statements that claims that one or more of those statements, called 'premises,' support another of them, called the 'conclusion.' Thus, every argument claims that its premises support its conclusion."[113] For example, William Lane Craig's cosmological argument for the existence of God is as follows:

Premise 1: Whatever begins to exist has a cause.

Premise 2: The universe began to exist.

Conclusion: Therefore, the universe has a cause.

In this argument, the two premises support the conclusion.

According to Henry Virkler, "An argument is a group of statements. A premise is a statement whose truthfulness is assumed to have been established already. A conclusion is a statement that allegedly follows from one or more premises

112 Thomas R. Schreiner, 1 Thomas R. Schreiner, 1, 2 Peter, Jude, The New American Commentary, vol. 37 (Nashville: Broadman & Holman Publishers, 2003), 175. vol. 37 (Nashville: Broadman & Holman Publishers, 2003), 175.

113 William Hughes, Jonathan Lavery, and Katheryn Doran, *Critical Thinking: An Introduction to the Basic Skills* (Ontario: Broadview Press, 2015), 4.

with logical certainty."[114] An argument has logical strength when its premises, if true, actually provide support for its conclusion. As stated by Hughes, Lavery, and Doran:

> The logical strength of an argument is independent of the truth or falsity of its premises: we do not need to know that the premises of an argument are true in order to assess its logical strength. When we assess the logical strength of an argument, we are really asking, *If the premises are true, would we be justified in accepting the conclusion?* And we can answer this question without knowing whether or not the premises actually are true.[115]

An argument that has both logical strength and true premises is called a "sound argument." As Hughes, Lavery, and Doran make clear, "If we want to know whether the conclusion of an argument is likely to be true, we need to know both that the argument is a strong one and that its premises are true."[116]

The first step in analyzing an argument is to identify the conclusion of the truth claim being made by the arguer. The following is a list of words or phrases that can help in identifying the conclusion:

---

114 Henry A. Virkler, *A Christian's Guide to Critical Thinking* (Eugene: Wipf & Stock Publishers, 2005), 178.
115 Hughes, Lavery, and Doran, *Critical Thinking*, 5.
116 Hughes, Lavery, and Doran, *Critical Thinking*, 7.

1. Consequently
2. Therefore
3. As a result
4. So
5. Clearly
6. It follows that
7. Accordingly
8. We may conclude
9. It entails
10. Hence
11. Thus
12. We may infer that
13. It must be that
14. It implies that
15. That is why

Once the conclusion of the argument has been identified, look for statements that provide supporting data or information for the conclusion. These statements will be the premises. The next step is to analyze the premises to determine if they are factual, reasonable, or valid. This is the point where the Christian can begin formulating his response.

Logical fallacies are committed all too often and are quite common while doing the work of defending the biblical worldview. To oversimplify, logical fallacies are logical errors in argumentation, reasoning, explanation, rhetoric, or debate. A logical fallacy is a flawed reasoning or false assumption that doesn't prove anything, even though it may seem to initially make sense on the surface. For example, someone may present the following argument: "The Bible was written by people, and people are not God. Therefore, the Bible cannot be the word of God." Here is how the argument would be diagrammed:

Premise 1: The Bible was written by people.

Premise 2: People are not God.

Conclusion: Therefore, the Bible is not God's word.

On the surface, the argument makes sense. The premises are true, and they seem to support the conclusion, but the faulty reasoning on the part of the arguer is not understanding the inspiration of the Scriptures—how the writers were moved by the Holy Spirit to write the very words of God.

Faulty reasoning is often employed in the attacks on the biblical worldview, and the Christian must be able to spot these errors in logic if they want to be able to respond in a way that not only refutes the attack but also creates an opportunity for sharing the truth of the gospel. Defending our hope in Christ presents no shortage of opportunities to present biblical truth, so it is imperative for the Christian to be equipped in every way possible to defend the faith against fallacious arguments.

Before entering in a discussion of twelve logical fallacies, this writer has encountered, while attempting to share the gospel, a brief description of how to formulate a response needs to be provided. First, when it is recognized that an individual is making a fallacious claim against the Christian worldview, the Christian should ask the person to explain his argument. This gives the Christian more information about what the arguer believes regarding the topic. Second, once the arguer has made an explanation, the Christian should ask him how he came to that conclusion; this lets the Christian know where the arguer got his information about the topic and helps in determining if his premises are true, reasonable, and valid. This is the point at which the Christian can begin refuting the argument by sharing evidence from the Bible that supports his biblical worldview.[117]

The following is an example of a response to a fallacious argument raised against the biblical worldview using the process mentioned above.[118] A Christian is attempting to share with an

---

117 These three steps are adopted from the book *Tactics: A Game Plan for Discussing Your Christian Convictions* by Gregory Koukl (Grand Rapids: Zondervan, 2009).

118 This example was heard in an online lecture presented by Dr. Vodie Baucham.

individual the Christian view on same-sex marriage, and he is using Leviticus 18:22 as the proof text for his position, "And you shall not lie with a male as one lies with a female; it is an abomination." The individual responds by attacking the Christian, a fallacy known as an "ad hominem" (more about this fallacy later). He says, "You Christians are such hypocrites because you love to pick and choose laws from the Bible." In response, the Christian asks him to explain what he means by that statement. The arguer responds with, "You are hypocrites because you only want to enforce the laws you agree with. You pick and choose your favorites." The Christian then asks, "How did you come to that conclusion?" The arguer responds, "Well, the Bible also says you are not to eat shellfish, but you do. So, you see, you pick and choose." His argument can be diagrammed as follows:

Premise 1: You Christians love to pick and choose laws from the Bible.

Premise 2: You eat shellfish, and the Bible says you can't.

Conclusion: Therefore, you Christians are hypocrites.

Premise 1 is where the Christian can begin the process of refuting the argument, for it is not true, reasonable, or valid. The Christian can begin his response by asking the question, "Have you ever given any thought to the fact that you are doing the same thing? I bet you would agree with Leviticus 19:11–18" (and the Christian should read those verses to him).

> You shall not steal, nor deal falsely, nor lie to one another. You shall not swear falsely by My name, so as to profane the name of your God; I am the Lord. You shall not oppress your neighbor, nor rob him. The wages of a hired man are not to remain with you all night until morning. You shall not curse a deaf man, nor place a stumbling block before the blind, but you shall revere your God; I am the Lord. You shall do no injustice in judgment; you shall not be partial to the poor nor defer to the great, but you are to judge your neighbor fairly. You shall not go about as a slanderer among your people, and you are not to act against the life of your neighbor; I am the Lord. You shall not hate your fellow countryman in your heart; you may surely reprove your neighbor, but shall not incur sin because of him. You shall not take vengeance, nor bear any grudge against the sons of your people, but you shall love your neighbor as yourself; I am the Lord.

"You pick and choose these laws to agree with but reject Leviticus 18:22. I know why I pick and choose. You see, God's laws are divided into three categories: (1) the moral law, which is for all time; (2) the civil law, which was for Israel living under a theocracy; and (3) the ceremonial law. The moral laws, of which Leviticus 18:22 is a part, are still for us to follow. So I know the basis for my picking and choosing; what is your basis? I know that I am a hypocrite; that's why I need a Savior. All of us are hypocrites, and that is why all of us need a Savior." The Christian has shown the arguer evidence from Scripture that supports his biblical worldview. This example demonstrates how by asking questions, the Christian can show the arguer that his argument has no basis in truth and may possibly create an opportunity for sharing the gospel.

The main objective of the process demonstrated above is to help the Christian identify the fallacy being used and then to formulate a response that may create an opportunity for sharing the gospel. However, the Christian must always keep in mind that the goal of critical thinking is not to win arguments but to reveal the truth of the gospel and to do so with "gentleness and reverence."

The following chapters present twelve of the fallacious arguments this writer has encountered while sharing the gospel. Several examples of each argument are described as well as an approach to refuting them. The goal is to demonstrate a process for refuting logical fallacies raised against the biblical worldview. It is not something that is easily grasped and will require practice. One helpful exercise is to practice analyzing arguments made in magazine articles, books, or the news media. Begin by determining the type of fallacy the arguer is using. Once that is determined, locate the conclusion the arguer has come to, in other words, his truth claim. Then locate his supporting data, his premises. Ask yourself, "Do his premises support his conclusion, and are they true?" Once you have spotted the error in his argument, practice formulating a response that would not only point out the error but also possibly open the door for sharing the gospel.

Chapter 5

CRITICAL THINKING AND THE BEGGING THE QUESTION FALLACY

———

The fallacy of "begging the question" is also known as "circular reasoning" or a "circular argument." Joel Mc-Durmon states, "It refers to an argument that assumes in its conclusion what it states as a premise of the argument.[119]" In other words, its premises presuppose, directly or indirectly, the truth of its conclusion. Take, for example, the following argument: The Bible is inspired by God, and the Bible says that God exists. Therefore, God exists. Notice the circular reasoning—premise 1: the Bible is inspired by God; premise 2: the Bible says God exists; conclusion: God exists. Premise 1 presupposes the conclusion. According to William Hughes, Jonathan Lavery, and Katheryn Doran, "Begging the question typically arises when we want to defend some claim yet have difficulty in finding reasons that will persuade others of its truth."[120] As an illustration, the following example is drawn

———

119 Joel McDurmon, *Biblical Logic In Theory & Practice* (Powder Springs: American Vision Press, 2011), 150.
120 Hughes, Lavery, and Doran, *Critical Thinking*, 116.

from an October 16, 2020, online article titled "What Does the Bible Really Say About Abortion?" by Dr. John Collins[121]. Collins states at the beginning of his article, "Christians who turn to Scripture to trump a political debate with the force of biblical authority should be reminded that the Bible does not actually say anything at all on the topic of abortion. On this issue, there is no divine revelation to be had."[122] In the article, Collins's argument outlines as follows:

Premise 1: The Bible provides no definitive ruling on abortion.

Premise 2: There is no law in the Bible forbidding the practice.

Premise 3: There is no discussion of abortion in the New Testament.

Conclusion: Therefore, there is no divine revelation on abortion.

In his argument, Collins's premises presuppose the truth of his conclusion; therefore, it is begging the question. The Christian's response to such an argument is to show the arguer, in

121   John J. Collins is Holmes Professor of Old Testament at Yale Divinity School.
122   John Collins, "What Does the Bible Really Say About Abortion?", *Religion News Service,* October 16, 2020, https://religionnews.com/2020/10/16/what-does-the-bible-really-say-about-abortion.

this case, Collins, the errors in his premises by asking questions such as, "Can you explain what you mean when you say the Bible provides no definitive ruling on abortion, and how you came to that conclusion?" In his article, Collins answers these questions. He begins by rebutting the pro-life claim of a right to life. He writes:

> The Bible's ambivalence on the subject of a right to life begins in its first book, Genesis. In chapter 9, God tells Noah after the flood: "Whoever sheds the blood of a human, by a human shall that person's blood be shed, for in his own image God made humankind." Since human beings are created in the image of God, life is protected, but the penalty for bloodshed is more bloodshed. God can even demand human sacrifice on occasion, most famously in the case of Abraham and Isaac, and the death penalty is routinely in the Bible for all sorts of offenses. The Bible, in fact, lacks any discourse of human rights. Life is a gift from God: The Lord giveth, and the Lord taketh away.[123]

Next, Collins responds to Christians who believe that their position on abortion stems from biblical teaching. He states, "In the entire corpus of biblical law, abortion is never mentioned."[124] He goes on to say:

---

123 Collins, "What Does the Bible Really Say?"
124 Collins, "What Does the Bible Really Say?"

Abortion was known, at least as a possibility, in Israel. The prophet Jeremiah curses the day he was born and the man who brought the news to his father, "because he did not kill me in the womb so my mother would have been my grave." Yet there is no law in the Bible forbidding the practice.[125]

Lastly, Collins defends his claim that there is no discussion of abortion in the New Testament with the following statement:

There is no discussion of abortion in the New Testament. The first explicit condemnations of abortion in Christian tradition appear in the second century CE in the Didache, a writing that claims to be based on the teachings of the apostles, and the Epistle of Barnabas, another early Christian work, modeled on the letters of Paul[126].

The evidence presented by Collins in support of his premises is faulty, as will be shown in the following paragraphs, therefore his truth claim is invalid. In his attack on the pro-life position of a right to life based upon Scripture, Collins states that in Scripture, the penalty for bloodshed is more bloodshed. This contradicts the Christian's claim. In response, the Christian should ask the question, "Have you ever given any thought to the reason why murder would be so grievous to God that He

---

125 Collins, "What Does the Bible Really Say?"
126 Collins, "What Does the Bible Really Say?"

would require life for life?" and then offer an explanation from Scripture.[127] A good starting place for the Christian would be the book of Genesis.

God required the death penalty for someone who took the life of another human being because all men (this includes women) are created in His "image"; Genesis 9:6, "Whoever sheds man's blood, by man his blood shall be shed, for in the image of God He made man." This "image" provides man with a unique status and explains why human life is specially protected, but animal life is not. It is because of man's special status among God's creation that this verse insists on the death penalty for murder.

As part of his evidence in support of his premises and how he came to his conclusion, Collins claims that at times God even called for a human sacrifice as in the case of Abraham and Isaac; Genesis 22:1-2:

Now it came about after these things, that God tested Abra-ham, and said to him, "Abraham!" And he said, "Here I am." He said, "Take now your son, your only son, whom you love, Isaac, and go to the land of Moriah, and offer him there as a burnt offering on one of the mountains of which

---

127 The explanation being offered in the following paragraphs is more than what a Christian would provide in his response to an argument such as this. It is given in such detail here for the purpose of demonstrating the need for the Christian to be prepared at all times to defend his faith.

I will tell you."

Once again, the Christian's response to Collins's explanation is to ask questions to find out the depth of his understanding of God's request of Abraham. For example, the Christian could ask, "Have you ever given any thought as to why God may have asked Abraham to do this, especially since God required life for life?" and then follow with an explanation using Scripture.

What Collins is overlooking is God's purpose in calling Abraham to sacrifice his son.[128] God never intended for Abraham to actually kill his son. God already knew what Abraham was willing to do. One of the purposes for which God called Abraham to sacrifice Isaac is found in John 8:56. Jesus said, "Your father Abraham rejoiced to see My day, and he saw it and was glad." Abraham longed to know God more intimately, to understand God's character and plan of salvation, and to comprehend and see the Savior. God instructed Abraham to sacrifice Isaac as a means to fulfill Abraham's desire of understanding, connecting with, empathizing with, knowing, and moving into greater intimacy with God. It was God's answer to Abraham's own request. In the agonizing struggle to sacri-

---

128 Tim Jennings, "Why Did God Tell Abraham to Kill Isaac?" Come and Reason Ministries, December 18, 2017, accessed January 2021, https://comeandreason.com/why-did-god-tell-abraham-to-kill-isaac/.

fice his son, Abraham identified with and gained insight into the heart of God.

A second purpose for which God called Abraham to sacrifice his son was for Abraham's character development. Abraham needed to choose to trust God and overcome his own fear, insecurity, and patterns of seeking to save himself. Abraham had feelings of fear that overruled his judgment, and on more than one occasion, he lied to protect himself. Consider his lie about Sarah being his sister.

Genesis 12:11–13:

It came about when he came near to Egypt, that he said to Sarai his wife, "See now, I know that you are a beautiful woman; and when the Egyptians see you, they will say, 'This is his wife'; and they will kill me, but they will let you live. Please say that you are my sister so that it may go well with me because of you, and that I may live on account of you."

Genesis 20:1–2:

"Now Abraham journeyed from there toward the land of the Negev, and settled between Kadesh and Shur; then he sojourned in Gerar. Abraham said of Sarah his wife, 'She is my sister.' So Abimelech king of Gerar sent and took Sarah."

Twice Abraham lied out of fear for his life. God had to bring Abraham to a decision point where he had to exercise his will, to choose to trust God, open his heart to the Spirit, and then choose to do what he knew was right in the face of powerful feelings tempting him to move in the opposite direction.

Abraham did choose to trust God in His directive to sacrifice his son.

Hebrews 11:17–19:

> By faith Abraham, when he was tested, offered up Isaac, and he who had received the promises was offering up his only begotten son; it was he to whom it was said, "In Isaac your descendants shall be called." He considered that God is able to raise people even from the dead, from which he also received him back as a type.

It did not seem logical to Abraham for God to ask him to kill his only son when God had said it would be through that son that He would give him numerous descendants. It could only be sorted out in Abraham's mind that God must intend to raise Isaac from the dead. Abraham "considered," a word meaning inward conviction and not merely an opinion.

To substantiate his claim that there is no law in the Bible forbidding the practice of abortion (premise 2), Collins uses the prophet Jeremiah as an example to indicate that abortion was known or at least a possibility in Israel. He writes, "The prophet Jeremiah curses the day he was born and the man who brought the news to his father, 'because he did not kill me in the womb so my mother would have been my grave.'"

Jeremiah 20:15:

"Cursed be the man who brought the news to my father, saying, 'A baby boy has been born to you!' And made him very happy."

Jeremiah 20:17:

"Because he did not kill me before birth, so that my mother would have been my grave, and her womb ever pregnant."

Here again, the Christian should ask the question, "Have you given any thought to the idea that Jeremiah wasn't speaking about abortion, that he was only speaking rhetorically?" Collins has taken Jeremiah's words out of context. Jeremiah's words have nothing to do with the possibility of an abortion. His words were a standard outcry made by people caught in calamity. Jeremiah, being troubled in his spirit, would have preferred to be stillborn or unborn. The reason is that God won't let him stop prophesying (Jeremiah 20:9), so he wishes instead that he had never been born. This is the only way he could have avoided his prophetic mission. Jeremiah was in great sorrow over watching his people reject God's word and the resulting judgment. If only he had not been called by God to prophesy was his cry.

In support of his premise that there is no law in the Bible forbidding the practice of abortion, Collins states:

> As far as abortion itself goes, the Jewish historian Josephus, writing at the end of the first century CE, claims that the Law of Moses—that is, the first five books of the Hebrew Bible or Old Testament—forbids abortion and regards it as infanticide, but there is no such law in the Bible.

As for the New Testament, Collins writes:

> There is no discussion of abortion in the New Testament. The first explicit condemnations of abortion in Christian tradition appear in the second century CE in the Didache, a writing that claims to be based on the teachings of the apostles, and the Epistle of Barnabas, another early Christian work, modeled on the letters of Paul.

Collins is using a logical fallacy called "argument from silence," which will be discussed in a later chapter. For now, an argument from silence attempts to demonstrate something as true in the absence of evidence or, more specifically, because of the lack of evidence. One thing that every Christian must deal with is the issue that Scripture doesn't record everything exhaustively. What the Scripture does do, however, is provide spiritual truths to help in determining the rightness or wrongness of an issue. In the case of abortion, the fact that men are created in the image of God (Genesis 9:6) and Exodus 20:13, "You shall not murder," convey the spiritual truth of a right to life for all who bear the image of God.

In analyzing Collins's argument, his premises are faulty, and therefore, the conclusion of his argument is not valid; it has no logical strength. He is correct in his view that the Bible does not mention abortion but is wrong in his statement that it does not say "anything at all" about the issue. As shown, the Bible does speak against the killing of an image-bearer of God, and even the child in the womb has that status. Jeremiah 1:5 states, "Before I formed you in the womb I knew you, and before you were born I consecrated you; I have appointed you a prophet to the nations." Before God formed Jeremiah in the womb, He knew him. The word "formed" comes from the Hebrew verb yatsar and is "...typically used to describe the process of shaping pottery. It appears in Genesis 2:7 as part of God's act of creating the first human from the dust of the earth."[129] The phrase "I knew you" comes from the Hebrew verb *yada* and "...is used to describe the most intimate

_____

129 John D. Barry et al., *Faithlife Study Bible* (Bellingham: Lexham Press, 2012, 2016), Jeremiah 1:5.

of relationships.[130]" The word "consecrated" comes from the Hebrew verb *qadash* and means "be holy, removed from common use."[131] Jeremiah was appointed by God as a prophet, set apart to be an image-bearer to the nations, while he was in the womb.

The Christian's response to an argument such as the one presented by Collins is to show the weakness in his premises by asking questions and using Scripture. Asking questions will help the Christian demonstrate to the arguer that his argument is circular, that he has assumed in the premises his conclusion making his argument invalid. In Collins's argument, he has assumed his conclusion in all three of his premises.

By asking questions, the Christian has demonstrated to the arguer that he is interested in his views and desires to keep the lines of communication open. It may also open the door for sharing more of the gospel.

In the book *Letter to a Christian Nation*, Sam Harris makes the following begging the question argument:

> If you think that it would be impossible to improve upon the Ten Commandments as a statement of morality, you really owe it to yourself to read some other scriptures. Once

130   Barry et al., *Faithlife Study*, Jeremiah 1:5.
131   Rick Brannan, ed., Lexham Research Lexicon of the Hebrew Bible, Lexham Research Lexicons (Bellingham: Lexham Press, 2020).

again, we need look no further than the Jains: Mahavira, the Jain patriarch, surpassed the morality of the Bible with a single sentence: "Do not injure, abuse, oppress, enslave, insult, torment, torture, or kill any creature or living being." Imagine how different our world might be if the Bible contained this as its central precept. Christians have abused, oppressed, enslaved, insulted, tormented, tortured, and killed people in the name of God for centuries, on the basis of a theologically defensible reading of the Bible. It is impossible to behave this way by adhering to the principles of Jainism. How, then, can you argue that the Bible provides the clearest statement of morality the world has ever seen?[132]

Harris's argument can be outlined as follows:

Premise 1: The Ten Commandments is not the best statement of morality.

Premise 2: Mahavira, the Jain patriarch, surpasses the morality of the Bible with one sentence.

Conclusion: Therefore, the Bible does not provide the clearest statement of morality the world has ever seen.

Harris has assumed in his conclusion what he states in premise 1 of his argument. In response, the Christian could make the

---

132 Sam Harris, Letter to a Christian Nation (New York: Vintage Books, 2006), 22–3.

following statement, "If I am hearing you correctly, you believe that it would be impossible for someone who is adhering to the principles of Jainism to act in an immoral way, but not so for a Christian adhering to the moral principles taught in the Bible. Can you tell me how you came to that conclusion?"

For Harris, the answer is found in the evidence he provides to support his premises. He states, "Christians have abused, oppressed, enslaved, insulted, tormented, tortured, and killed people in the name of God for centuries, on the basis of a theologically defensible reading of the Bible." The Christian could then ask, "Have you ever given any thought to the fact that the immoral actions of a few people who claim to be Christians do not invalidate the high moral standards taught in the Bible? Have you given any thought to the idea that a Christian committed to the truth of God's Word would desire to live by that standard?" The Christian can now, using Scripture, provide a response to Harris that points out the weakness in his claim.

The Christian can begin by stating that the Bible regards any kind of abuse as sin because the Christian is commanded to love one another. (John 13:34, "A new commandment I give to you, that you love one another, even as I have loved you, that you also love one another.") Abuse disregards others and is the opposite of this command. An abuser desires to satisfy his natural selfishness regardless of the consequences to himself or others. Oppression, enslaving, insulting, tormenting, torturing, and killing are all forms of abuse and are the opposite of the command to love.

A person who truly loves God and is walking in His Spirit cannot, as a way of life, treat others immorally.

Ephesians 4:32,

"Be kind to one another, tender-hearted, forgiving each other, just as God in Christ also has forgiven you."

Galatians 5:16,

"But I say, walk by the Spirit, and you will not carry out the desire of the flesh."

Out of his fear of bad karma, the Jainist may not involve himself in the immoral acts mentioned in the argument by Harris. The Christian may not involve himself in those acts out of God's command to love. The Jainist out of fear, the Christian out of love. The Apostle John writes in 1 John 4:18, "There is no fear in love; but perfect love casts out fear, because fear involves punishment, and the one who fears is not perfected in love." In this verse, John seeks to instill in the heart of the believer that the person who fears lacks love. Unbelief leaves a person disturbed, but the love of God soothes the heart. All

Christians must actively exercise this love in daily life. Love is better than fear, so it is difficult to accept Harris's argument that an individual following the principles of Jainism is less likely to commit immoral acts than one following the principles taught in the Bible. Harris has presented no evidence to validate his claim. The premises of Harris's argument do not support his conclusion; instead, he assumes his conclusion in his premises, making his argument circular or begging the question.

A personal experience with this type of argument occurred during a street witnessing event when sharing with an unbeliever John 3:16, "For God so loved the world that He gave His only begotten Son that whoever believes in Him shall not perish but have eternal life." In response, the unbeliever presented the following begging the question argument: "How can you say that God is a loving God when in the Old Testament He commands the annihilation of Canaanites?" His argument outlines as follows:

Premise 1: God is not loving.

Premise 2: In the Old Testament, God commands the annihilation of the Canaanites.

Conclusion: Therefore, God is not loving.

In his argument, the arguer has assumed in his conclusion

what he states in premise 1, making it a begging the question fallacy. In responding to this argument, the arguer was first asked to explain why he believes God's command to kill the Canaanites demonstrates that He is an unloving God. After listening to his explanation, he was asked a follow-up question, "Is God arbitrary, or does He give reasons for judging people in the Old Testament?" Following his answer, the arguer was asked a final question, "Have you ever given any thought to the fact that God may have had a reason for judging the Canaanites?" The arguer was then offered three possible reasons for God judging the Canaanites: (1) The Canaanites were occupying the land of which Israel had legal ownership—and without consent of the owner. (2) In spite of having a legal title and a divinely approved claim on the land, Abram and his descendants could not take immediate and total occupation of the land. They had to wait until the "sin of the Amorites" had "reached its full measure" (Genesis 15:16). This passage seems to say that the nature of the Amorite/Canaanite society in Abraham's day was not yet so wicked as to justify God acting in such a comprehensive judgment upon it. The wickedness of the Canaanites was not trivial. The most exhaustive list of the kinds of wickedness comes from Leviticus 18. It chronicles incest, adultery, bestiality, ritual prostitution, and homosexual acts, and most significantly, Deuteronomy 12:29–31 singles out child sacrifice as particularly abhorrent. (3) Deuteronomy 20 warns that if the Israelites follow the practice of taking captives and integrating them into the Israelite community, "…they will not teach you to follow all the detestable things they do in worshiping their gods, and you would sin against the Lord Your God" (20:18).

Even though the arguer did not accept any one of the three reasons, by responding in such a manner, he was shown that God did have a justifiable reason for commanding the killing of the Canaanites. Also, by responding with gentleness and reverence, there was the opportunity to share more of the message of Jesus Christ.

At this point, some of you may be saying, "Okay, I see how the argument is classified as begging the question and how the arguer was shown the error of his statement, but this is something I could never do. I do not know the Bible well enough to be able to respond in the way you did." I hear that same reasoning from many Christians, and it illustrates the importance of having a comprehensive discipleship training program within the church.

A typical discipleship training program usually focuses on the following areas: (1) new believers, (2) experiencing God, (3) prayer, (4) missions and evangelism, (5) Bible book studies, and (6) studies that focus on building Christian families. A more comprehensive program would include training in apologetics and critical thinking. A list of websites containing resources to assist in developing discipleship training in these two areas is found in Chapter 17.

Chapter 6

CRITICAL THINKING AND THE STRAW MAN FALLACY

The straw man fallacy is an argument that distorts an opposing view in order to make it easier to attack. The person using the straw man pretends to attack their opponents' view while, in reality, they are actually attacking a distorted version of that view. In doing so, they conclude that they have refuted their opponent's position. According to Hughes, Lavery, and Doran, the straw man fallacy "…usually arises in debates over controversial issues when one side is attempting to avoid or deflect criticisms presented by the other side."[133]

In the book The God Delusion, Richard Dawkins presented the following straw man argument in an attempt to defeat the Christian's claim of the existence of an all-loving God.

Argument:

The God of the Old Testament is arguably the most unpleasant character in all of fiction: jealous and proud of it; a petty,

---

133 Hughes, Lavery, and Doran, *Critical Thinking,* 116.

unjust, unforgiving control-freak; a vindictive, bloodthirsty ethnic cleanser; a misogynistic, homophobic, racist, infanticidal, genocidal, filicidal, pestilential, megalomaniacal, sadomasochistic, capriciously malevolent bully.[134]

Premise 1: God is the most unpleasant character in all of fiction.

Premise 2: God is jealous and proud of it; a petty, unjust, unforgiving control freak; a vindictive, bloodthirsty ethnic cleanser; a misogynistic, homophobic, racist, infanticidal, genocidal, filicidal, pestilential, megalomaniacal, sadomasochistic, capriciously malevolent bully.

Conclusion: Therefore, God, if He exists, is not loving.

In this argument, Dawkins makes the assertion, a straw man, that God's character is the way he says (premise 2). Dawkins draws his inaccurate description of God from his interpretation of events recorded in the Bible. This God is fictional and does not exist; therefore, the loving God described by the Christian does not exist. He never deals with what Christians actually believe, and the Bible teaches, about the nature and attributes of God. By making this straw man, Dawkins believes he has defeated the argument for the existence of a

134 Richard Dawkins, *The God Delusion* (New York: HoughtonMifflin, 2006), 31.

loving God.

To counter a straw man argument such as this, the Christian should ask questions that will help clarify the difference between the real truth and the straw man imposter, then emphasize that the real truth still stands regardless of the straw man. For example, the Christian could ask Dawkins, "What do you mean when you say God is an 'unforgiving control freak,' and how did you come to that conclusion?" Dawkins might respond to the questions with some examples from the Old Testament of God exercising His control and power over people. The Christian could then respond with a statement such as: "Have you ever given any thought to the fact that if He is the Creator of all things, He should have the right to control them just as you would have the right to do whatever you desire with things you might create? Control is not an anxiety or a lust God has; it is just part of His nature as God. As for Him being unforgiving, let's look at a few passages of Scripture that show Him giving second and third chances to many undeserving people." In responding this way, the Christian has pointed out Dawkins's straw man and has done so in a way that may have created an opportunity for sharing more of the gospel.

In a discussion about the Bible being the perfect word of an omniscient deity, Sam Harris makes the following straw man argument:

> With the eyes of faith, you can discover magical prescience in any text. I literally walked into the cookbook aisle of a bookstore, randomly opened a cookbook, found a recipe for, I think it was, wok-seared shrimp with ogo relish or something, and then came up with a mystical interpretation of the recipe. Anyone can do this. You can play connect-the-dots with any crazy text and find wisdom in it.[135]

Premise 1: You can discover magical prescience in any text.

Premise 2: I came up with a mystical interpretation of the recipe for wok-seared shrimp.

Conclusion: Therefore, the Bible is not the perfect word of an omniscient deity.

Harris's straw man is his mystical interpretation of the recipe for wok-seared shrimp. By demonstrating the absurdity of such a claim, he believes that he has defeated the Christian's claim that the Bible is the perfect word of an omniscient deity.

Here is how the straw man fallacy is accomplished:

---

135 Christopher Hitchens, Richard Dawkins, Sam Harris, and Daniel Dennett, *The Four Horsemen* (New York: Random House, 2019), 78.

1. The real argument is ignored (the Christian's claim that the Bible is the perfect word of an omniscient deity).

2. A pretend argument (straw man) is established (mystical interpretation of the recipe for wok-seared shrimp).

3. The pretend argument is attacked and defeated (the absurdity of such a claim).

4. Victory over the real argument is claimed.

There are three main strategies a Christian can use in responding to straw man arguments: (1) The Christian can point out the straw man to the arguer by explaining how his argument distorts His original statement (the Christian's claim that the Bible is the perfect word of an omniscient deity). Here is where the Christian can use the question: Can you explain what you mean by that statement (you can discover magical prescience in any text) because it does not address my position; instead, it distorts it? This will put the arguer on the defensive by having him justify why he believes his statement is the same as that of the Christian. (2) The Christian can ignore the straw man and continue to share evidence/proof for his view. (3) The Christian can accept the straw man and, instead of arguing in favor of his view, defend the distorted version presented by the arguer. This is not a very good choice, however, for by choosing to defend the straw man, the Christian can give the impression that it is truly his view.

The best approach is number one. In Harris's argument, the Christian should have him explain what he means by his statement and how he came to his conclusion. In the process, the Christian can then point out to Harris that his view is actually a distortion of the one he presented and that his straw man did not defeat the claim that the Bible is the perfect word of an omniscient deity. That truth still stands.

After making the truth claim that the God of the Bible is all-powerful, all-good, and all-loving in a street witnessing event, a person within the crowd that had gathered presented the following straw man argument: "If an all-powerful and all-good God existed, He would not allow so much evil in the world."

Premise 1: An all-powerful, all-good, and all-loving God would not allow evil.

Premise 2: Evil exists.

Conclusion: Therefore, God does not exist.

The arguer has presented the claim that an all-loving and all-powerful God would not allow evil. This is his straw man. Since evil exists, he believes he has defeated his straw man; therefore, my claim of the existence of an all-loving and all-powerful God is defeated as well. For many people, the existence of evil seems inconsistent with our belief in God's goodness or omniscience or power. This has led them to conclude that the existence of evil in the world makes it unlikely that God exists.

Here is a condensed version of how the conversation went with the individual making the claim that since evil exists, God cannot exist:

Me: Can you explain what you mean by that statement?

Arguer: Well, if God was all good, He would only want what is good for us, and evil is not good.

Me: How do you define good?

Arguer: "Good" is what helps us enjoy life. An all-good God would want us to enjoy life.

Me: How would you describe evil?

Arguer: Anything that takes our joy, our happiness, away from life.

Me: What standard are you using to differentiate between evil and good? It can't be your own standard because if it were, the standards would be different for each person. Have you ever given any thought to the idea that what we might consider evil, God intended it for some ultimate good? Take, for example, the Old Testament story of Joseph and his brothers in Genesis 50:20, "As for you, you meant evil against me, but God meant it for good in order to bring about this present result, to preserve many people alive." Or consider the evil actions of the men who crucified our Lord. It was an evil act, but it has turned out for good to the world.

Even though the arguer realized his straw man was defeated, he still had questions about the existence of evil, but the conversation brought him to a point where he was open to hearing more of the gospel.

Chapter 7
CRITICAL THINKING AND THE AD HOMINEM FALLACY

A n ad hominem fallacy is an attack on the person making the argument rather than attacking the argument itself. By focusing on the person instead of the argument, the fallacy diverts attention away from the real issue. The following example of an ad hominem fallacy occurred during a debate between apologist James White and the Bible critic Dr. Bart Ehrman.[136] In this debate, James White argued that God had preserved His Word in the multiplicity of fragmented manuscripts (five thousand plus to date), even though many of those manuscripts contain differences. Though in many pieces, the "tenacity" of the Word remains. In essence, he argued that it is like having 1,010 pieces for a thousand-piece jigsaw puzzle. It's all there; we just have more than we need. Amidst his rebuttals of this claim, Dr. Ehrman complained that only Evangelical scholars continue to make this "tenacity" argument (against the weight of international scholarly opinion),

---

136   The example was taken from McDurmon's book (pages 318–19).

and Evangelicals do so because they must defend their underlying doctrine of inspiration. In other words, his argument was, "You only believe that because you have a vested interest in doing so: your evangelical religious tenets require you to do so at the expense of truth." This dismissal was merely an attack on Dr. White because of his self-interest in the reliability of the Bible; it did not address the issue itself. Here is how Ehrman's argument flows:

> Premise 1: Evangelicals continue to make this argument at the expense of truth.
>
> Premise 2: Evangelicals do so because they must defend their underlying doctrine of inspiration.
>
> Conclusion: Therefore, you only believe it because your evangelical tenants require you to do so.

There are actually four categories of the ad hominem fallacy. (1) There is the circumstantial ad hominem fallacy, which suggests that the person who is making the argument is biased or predisposed to take a particular stance, and therefore, the argument is unnecessarily invalid. In other words, it is assumed that the argument is wrong because of the self-interest of the one making the argument. The argument presented above is an example of this type of ad hominem attack. (2) This is the guilt by association ad hominem attack. This occurs when the source is viewed negatively because of its association with another person or group who is already viewed negatively. An example of this type of ad hominem fallacy would be to discredit your view of the Bible's reliability because you are a southern Baptist. (3) There is the tu quoque (Latin for "you also") ad hominem fallacy. It is also called an appeal to hypocrisy. You are saying something but doing just the opposite—however, it makes no impact on the validity of the argument. For example, someone makes the argument that smoking is bad for you, but they continue to smoke. (4) The last category of the ad hominem fallacy is the abusive type. This occurs when the person is attacked rather than the argument.[137]

There are four ways of responding to an ad hominem fallacy. First, the Christian can point out the irrelevance of the attack. He can do this by explaining that the personal attack has nothing to do with the discussion at hand. Second, he can respond to the attack directly. Ask the arguer to explain his statement and how he came to that conclusion. The Christian can then share Scripture with the arguer that supports the biblical worldview. Third, the Christian can ignore the attack.

---

137   Bo Barrett, "Lecture Section 2: Ad Hominem," in *Mastering Logical Fallacies*, 2015 (San Francisco, CA: Udemy, 2015), accessed online April 2020, https://www.udemy.com/course/mastering-logical-fallacies/learn/lecture/6136170?start=0#overview.

He can choose to keep the discussion going while refusing to engage with the personal attack. Fourth, the Christian can acknowledge the attack and move on.

An example from the Bible is found in John 8:42–48:

> Jesus said to them, "If God were your Father, you would love Me, for I proceeded forth and have come from God, for I have not even come on My own initiative, but He sent Me. Why do you not understand what I am saying? It is because you cannot hear My word. You are of your father the devil, and you want to do the desires of your father. He was a murderer from the beginning and does not stand in the truth because there is no truth in him. Whenever he speaks a lie, he speaks from his own nature, for he is a liar and the father of lies. But because I speak the truth, you do not believe Me. Which one of you convicts Me of sin? If I speak truth, why do you not believe Me? He who is of God hears the words of God; for this reason, you do not hear them, because you are not of God." The Jews answered and said to Him, "Do we not say rightly that You are a Samaritan and have a demon?"

Rather than respond to Jesus's charge that they were "not of God but of their father the devil" with reason, the Pharisees resorted to the ad hominem fallacy. They attacked Jesus and said He was a Samaritan and had a demon. Jesus could have used the first response and pointed out to the Pharisees that their personal attack on Him was not relevant to the discussion about their relationship with God. Jesus could have used the third strategy and ignored the attack and just moved on with His teaching. He could have also chosen to use the fourth strategy and acknowledged their attack and then moved on; this, however, He could not do because it would be admitting that He had a demon. Instead, Jesus chose to use the second strategy and respond to the attack directly and then support His claim with Scripture, which is clearly displayed in John 8:49–58:

Jesus answered, "I do not have a demon; but I honor My Father, and you dishonor Me. But I do not seek My glory; there is One who seeks and judges. Truly, truly, I say to you, if anyone keeps My word he will never see death." The Jews said to Him, "Now we know that You have a demon. Abraham died, and the prophets also; and You say, 'If anyone keeps My word, he will never taste of death.' Surely You are not greater than our father Abraham, who died? The prophets died too; whom do You make Yourself out to be?" Jesus answered, "If I glorify Myself, My glory is nothing; it is My Father who glorifies Me, of whom you say, 'He is our God'; and you have not come to know Him, but I know Him; and if I say that I do not know Him, I will be a liar like you, but I do know Him and keep His word. Your father Abraham rejoiced to see My day, and he saw it and was glad." So the Jews said to Him, "You are not yet fifty years old, and have You seen Abraham?" Jesus said to them, "Truly, truly, I say to you, before Abraham was born, I am."

In verse 49, Jesus responded directly to the claim of the Pharisees that He had a demon. In verses 50–51, Jesus was indirectly asking them how they came to their conclusion by stating that He does not seek His own glory: "There is only One who seeks and judges, and that is God. Therefore, how did you arrive at the conclusion that I had a demon or was a Samaritan?" They responded to Jesus's statement in verses 52–53. Then Jesus uses Scripture to defend His truth statement as to who He is by referring to Abraham rejoicing to see His day (verses 56 and 58). Eli Lizorkin-Eyzenberg explains:

> Jesus made a stunning statement here in response to the challenge given by the Ioudaioi. He said that Abraham met Him and when he did, he rejoiced. We can already anticipate the reaction of those who opposed Him. What Jesus said was absolutely true. In fact, Abraham saw the incarnate Logos of God several times. Take one concrete example. This event took place immediately prior to Abraham's negotiations with God over the salvation of the city of Sodom because of the righteousness of some of Sodom's residents. You will remember that three visitors came to Abraham. Two were angels and the third was the LORD in human

form (Genesis 18:1–33). The Torah seems to be completely unapologetic about this kind of encounter between God and men when God appears in human form as in Genesis 18 or in Genesis 32.[138]

The argument from the religious leaders can be diagrammed as follows:

Premise 1: Abraham is our father (8:39).

Premise 2: Abraham died and the prophets also, and You say, "If anyone keeps My word, he will never taste of death" (8:52).

Premise 3: Surely You are not greater than our father Abraham, who died? (8:53)

Conclusion: Therefore, You are a Samaritan and have a demon.[139]

A personal experience with this type of argument occurred during an airline flight when attempting to explain the gospel to the passenger in the next seat. After quoting 1 John 1:9, "If we confess our sins, He is faithful and righteous to forgive us

---

138 Eli Lizorkin-Eyzenberg, *The Jewish Gospel of John*. Tel Aviv: Jewish Studies for Christians, 2015, Kindle, location 3250.
139 Samaritans were regarded by Jews as half-breed heretics who also (at least later) were associated with demonic/cultic magic. (Gerald L. Borchert, John 1–11, *The New American Commentary*, vol. 25A [Nashville: Broadman & Holman Publishers, 1996], 307.)

our sins and to cleanse us from all unrighteousness," the passenger presented the following ad hominem argument, "You Christians think you are so righteous. But look at your history and how you murdered innocent people through the Inquisition, the Salem Witch Trials, and the Crusades. You are not as righteous as you think you are."

Premise 1: You think you are so righteous because you are a Christian.

Premise 2: You Christians murdered innocent people through the Inquisition, the Salem Witch Trials, and the Crusades.

Conclusion: Therefore, Christians are not so righteous.

The best approach to take in responding to an ad hominem argument such as the one presented above is to point out the irrelevance of the attack (approach 1). It was explained to the passenger how that his attack on Christians was irrelevant and had nothing to do with the truth claim that if we confess our sins, Jesus will forgive us our sins and cleanse us from all unrighteousness. In the explanation, he was told that the un-Christian actions of a few do not negate the reality of the righteousness achieved through Christ. Through the explanation, he saw the error of his attack, and that opened up the opportunity for sharing more of the gospel.

Chapter 8

CRITICAL THINKING AND THE APPEAL TO AUTHORITY FALLACY

—

According to McDurmon:

> A fallacious appeal to authority attempts to persuade by leveraging expertise, tradition, boasted credentials, fame, social status, celebrity, etc., when these characteristics do not necessarily pertain to the issue at hand. Even when cited authorities have legitimate expertise in the topic, their expertise itself does not guarantee the truth of the argument under discussion.[140]

Henry Virkler provides three reasons why an appeal to authority may not guarantee the truth of an argument:[141]

1. The authority may be misquoted, either intentionally or unintentionally.

2. In an age when knowledge is growing so rapidly, even competent people are not always well-informed on all matters within their general area of expertise.

---

140 McDurmon, *Biblical Logic*, 245–46.
141 Virkler, *Christian's Guide*, 191–92.

3. There are often significant differences of opinion among experts on various issues. Therefore, quoting only one authority while not admitting that there are other points of view may lead to the inaccurate conclusion that there is consensus on issues when there is not.

In the book *The God Delusion,* Dawkins makes the following claim, "If our moral sense, like our sexual desire, is rooted in our deep Darwinian past, predating religion, we should expect that research on the human mind would reveal some moral universals, crossing geographical and cultural barriers, and also, crucially, religious barriers."[142] To support his claim, Dawkins appeals to a former Harvard professor, Marc D. Hauser, who wrote the book *Moral Minds: How Nature Designed Our Universal Sense of Right and Wrong.* The problem is Hauser's studies were based on animal cognition as a window into the evolution of the human mind, but there is more. In 2011, Hauser resigned from Harvard after being found guilty of falsifying and fabricating his data. Details of his misconduct were documented in a September 5, 2012, *Boston Globe* article titled "Ex-Harvard scientist fabricated, manipulated data, report says," written by Carolyn Johnson.[143] This is why using an appeal to authority to support an argument is not always

142 Dawkins, *The God Delusion,* 222.
143 Carolyn Y. Johnson, "Ex-Harvard scientist fabricated, manipulated data, report says," *Boston Globe,* September 5, 2012.

the best approach; if the authority falls, so does the argument.

The following is an example of an appeal to authority taken from John 7:40–43:

> Some of the people therefore, when they heard these words, were saying, "This certainly is the Prophet." Others were saying, "This is the Christ." Still others were saying, "Surely the Christ is not going to come from Galilee, is He? Has not the Scripture said that the Christ comes from the descendants of David, and from Bethlehem, the village where David was?" So a division occurred in the crowd because of Him.

The argument can be diagrammed as follows:

> Premise 1: Jesus comes from Galilee.
>
> Premise 2: Scriptures say that the Christ will come from the descendants of David and from Bethlehem.
>
> Conclusion: Therefore, Jesus cannot be the Christ.

The appeal to authority can be seen in the appeal the people made to the Scriptures in support of their belief that Jesus could not be the Messiah. They were correct in their understanding that the Messiah would come from David's line as told in 2 Samuel 7:12 and Psalm 98:3–4 and that He would come from Bethlehem as prophesied in Micah 5:2. What made their argument a fallacious appeal to authority was that they did not know the One with whom they made the argument. If they had bothered to investigate, to ask questions of Him, they would have discovered that He was of the lineage of David and that He was born in Bethlehem. This is a mistake that is sometimes made by those with whom a Christian may be sharing the gospel. The unbeliever may not be well informed enough about the gospel, which could lead him into making a fallacious appeal to authority in order to refute the Christian's message.

As a personal example, while carrying on a conversation about the Bible with a group of young people during a street witnessing event, one individual made the following claim, "The Bible is full of contradictions and discrepancies." When asked, "How did you come to that conclusion?" the person stated, "Our American literature professor in college told us." The person was then asked if he could provide an example of a discrepancy or contradiction, and he said that he could not. The final question asked was, "Have you ever read the Bible?" and he answered, "No." The arguer's appeal to authority was his American literature professor, who may or may not have been knowledgeable enough about the Bible to make such a claim. His argument can be diagrammed as follows:

Premise 1: My college professor said that the Bible is full of contradictions and discrepancies.

Conclusion: Therefore, the Bible cannot be trusted.

The following is an example of an appeal to authority from one of the social issues facing our culture today, same-sex marriage. In a December 5, 2008, online Newsweek article titled "Gay Marriage: Our Mutual Joy," the author Lisa Miller uses several examples of a fallacious appeal to authority in support of her view of same-sex marriage. Here is one of her arguments:

Paul was tough on homosexuality, though recently progressive scholars have argued that his condemnation of men who "were inflamed with lust for one another" (which he calls "a perversion") is really a critique of the worst kind of wickedness: self-delusion, violence, promiscuity and debauchery. In his book "The Arrogance of Nations," the scholar Neil Elliott argues that Paul is referring in this famous passage to the depravity of the Roman emperors, the craven habits of Nero and Caligula, a reference his audience would have grasped instantly. "Paul is not talking about what we call homosexuality at all," Elliott says. "He's talking about a certain group of people who have done everything in this list. We're not dealing with anything like gay love or gay marriage. We're talking about really, really violent people who meet their end and are judged by God." In any case, one might add, Paul argued more strenuously against divorce—and at least half of the Christians in America disregard that teaching.[144]

Miller's argument can be diagrammed as follows:

Premise 1: The Apostle Paul is not speaking of homosexuals in Romans 1:27–32.

Premise 2: Dr. Neil Elliott argues that Paul is referring to the depravity of the Roman emperors.

Conclusion: Therefore, Paul is not dealing with anything like gay love or gay marriage.

Miller's appeal to authority is Neil Elliott, a New Testament scholar, teacher, and Episcopal priest. But he is just one scholar, and many others could be called who could refute his views on Paul. In response to the article, Dr. Albert Mohler writes:

Miller picks her sources carefully. She cites Neil Elliott but never balances his argument with credible arguments from another scholar, such as Robert Gagnon of Pittsburgh Theological Seminary. Her scholarly sources are chosen so that they all offer an uncorrected affirmation of her argument.[145]

144 Lisa Miller, "Gay Marriage: Our Mutual Joy," Newsweek, December 5, 2008, https://www.newsweek.com/gay-marriage-our-mutual-joy-83287.
145 Albert Mohler, "Newsweek Argues the Religious Case for Gay Marriage," Christian Headlines, December 10, 2008, https://www.christianheadlines.com/news/newsweek-argues-the-religious-case-for-gay-

In responding to a fallacious appeal to authority, the Christian should ask the arguer if he knew how the authority came to his conclusion and what were the sources used by the authority. In the Dawkins example, he could have been misquoting his source, or now that it is known that his source falsified his research data, it could be used to show that Dawkins's appeal to this authority is invalid. Asking questions about the expert and their conclusions will assist the Christian in preparing a response to the fallacious appeal to authority.

Another personal experience with this type of argument occurred during one of our outreach events. After making the following truth claim, "God, at a specific point in time in actual human history, chose to become incarnate, a human being, took on a full human nature while remaining God," an individual attending the event presented the following appeal to authority argument, "How can you prove this? The validity of a claim such as this should be tested by scientific standards because science is a standard the majority of people agree on."

In this example, the authority being appealed to is the "majority of people." The argument is as follows:

Premise 1: Christian truth claims should be tested against a standard.

Premise 2: Science is the standard the majority of people agree on.

marriage-11596776.html.

Conclusion: Therefore, Christian truth claims should be tested by science.

The arguer was asked, "Are the majority of people experts in Christian truth claims or in the use of the scientific standard? What scientific standards are you referring to? Can all Christian truth claims be tested against a scientific standard?" The answers were unknown by the arguer, and therefore, the premises of his argument were invalid, making his argument unsound. In responding in this way, the arguer was shown the error in his statement, and he was then shown evidence from Scripture that supported the truth claims about Jesus.

Chapter 9

CRITICAL THINKING AND THE APPEAL TO IGNORANCE AND ARGUMENT FROM SILENCE FALLACIES

Appeal to Ignorance

The appeal to ignorance involves drawing a conclusion on the basis of the absence of evidence against the conclusion. According to McDurmon:

> The appeal to ignorance attempts to establish a proposition based on lack of knowledge. This fallacy commits the basic error of assuming that an absence of evidence equals evidence of absence, or the absence of proof means proof of absence. Primarily, we must account for the limitations of human knowledge. You cannot legitimately move from the fact of "no evidence found" to say, "no evidence exists." Even if every person in history searched the world over for the duration of their lives over multiple generations and still found no "evidence," this would not prove that no evidence exists, for the simple fact that the universe is infinitely larger (and infinitely smaller) than the sum total of all human experience. To make a definitive claim that no evidence exists, you must be able to search every corner of the universe

simultaneously at every moment. It is impossible, therefore, to prove such a negative claim unless you possess omni-science and omnipresence.[146]

This fallacy is not about an ignorant person; rather, it is when an individual mistakenly believes that something must be false because it has not been proven true or that something must be true because it has not been proven false. Here are a few examples:

1. You cannot prove God does not exist; therefore, God exists.

2. You cannot prove God exists, so God does not exist.

3. You cannot prove vegetables are not sentient, so we should treat them as if they are sentient.

4. You cannot prove that we will not create strong artificial intelligence in the future; therefore, we will.

5. Scientists, writing a book about life, state the following, "Life began somewhere else in the universe and was sent here by rocketships in the form of micro-organisms by a higher civilization...I know this sounds ridiculous, and maybe it isn't true, but you can't prove that it isn't."

146 McDurmon, *Biblical Logic*, 258.

Be skeptical whenever someone attempts to prove a claim by using your inability to disprove one. Be skeptical when people use a lack of understanding (i.e., ignorance) to make a claim about reality. Be suspicious whenever someone says, "Well, you cannot prove it is not true!" The burden of proof is upon the one making the claim, so in response to a fallacious argument such as this, ask the questions, "How did you come to that conclusion? What evidence do you have?"

Sam Harris presents the following appeal to ignorance argument:

> Finding ourselves in a universe that seems bent on destroying us, we quickly discover, both as individuals and as societies, that it is a good thing to understand the forces arrayed against us. And so it is that every human being comes to desire genuine knowledge about the world. This has always posed a special problem for religion, because every religion preaches the truth of propositions for which it has no evidence. In fact, every religion preaches the truth of propositions for which no evidence is even "conceivable." This put the "leap" in Kierkegaard's leap of faith.[147]

Harris's argument outlines as follows:

Premise 1: Every human being comes to desire genuine

---

147 Sam Harris, *The End of Faith* (New York: W. W. Norton & Company, 2004), 23.

knowledge about the world.

Premise 2: Religion preaches the truth of propositions for which no evidence is even conceivable.

Conclusion: Therefore, religion requires a "leap of faith" to understand truths about the world.

Harris's argument involves drawing a conclusion on the basis of an absence of evidence against the conclusion. It is his belief that Christians are using Kierkegaard's concept of "leap of faith"[148] when seeking to understand the world in which they live because the Bible, the source for their worldview, is full of unprovable propositions about life. This demonstrates Harris's lack of biblical knowledge making his argument an appeal to ignorance.

The questions that could be asked of Harris are: Can you explain what you mean by "truth of propositions"? What propositions are you referring to? How did you come to the conclusion that there is no conceivable evidence for the truth of the propositions presented in the Bible? Asking questions such as these will enable the Christian to understand the basis for Harris's argument and demonstrate to him that he is interested in his reasoning. Harris's answers may show that he

148 Kierkegaard's concept of leap points to a state in which a person is faced with a choice that cannot be justified rationally, and he, therefore, has to leap into it.

is unaware of the evidence for the truth claims of the Bible, and the Christian can share such evidence and, in the process, point out the errors in his argument. By asking questions and responding with gentleness and reverence, the Christian has possibly opened the door for sharing more of the gospel.

Premise 1: Evolution is a proven scientific fact.

Premise 2: Darwin demonstrated in his book *The Origin of Species* that you do not need to invoke the supernatural to explain how life on earth began.

Conclusion: Therefore, evolution, unlike creationism, does not require a leap of faith to understand how life began.

In response to this appeal to ignorance fallacy, the Christian should first ask the arguer to explain what he means when he states that evolution is a proven scientific fact. The Christian should listen carefully to the arguer's answer and then follow with a statement such as, "Did you know that, contrary to popular belief, there is no such thing as scientific proof? Proofs exist only in mathematics and logic, not in science. Science is empirical and based upon the interpretation of gathered data to a proposition and is subject to researcher bias and misinterpretation."

The next question for the Christian to ask would be, "How

did you come to your conclusion that evolution does not require a leap of faith because it is based on fact?" The arguer might possibly respond with Darwin's finches found in the Galapagos Islands or the peppered moths of Industrial England as his evidence. The Christian could agree that the finches and moths did change, but that in the change, the finches were still birds, and the moths were still moths. There was no change from one "kind" of animal to another.

The next question to be asked of the arguer is, "Can you provide one example of a change in 'kind'?" The answer, of course, is no. There is nothing in the fossil record to support such a change. The only source the arguer has is what his teachers/professors have told him. Therefore, he is doing what he claims the Christian is doing, taking a leap of faith. As Richard Dawkins was quoted as saying, "Faith is the great cop-out, the great excuse to evade the need to think and evaluate evidence. Faith is belief in spite of, even perhaps because of, the lack of evidence." The argument from ignorance is that the arguer doesn't know that his proof can be proven false. Science has not proven evolution, and Darwin's book has not demonstrated the truth about the origin of species. He may not even be aware of the difference between macro and microevolution.[149]

149 Macroevolution is evolution on a large scale, above the species level, over a long period of time that results in new species. Microevolution is simply a change in gene frequency within a population. Evolution at this scale can be observed over short periods of time.

An example of an appeal to ignorance from the Bible is found in John 1:45–50:

Philip found Nathanael and said to him, "We have found Him of whom Moses in the Law and also the Prophets wrote—Jesus of Nazareth, the son of Joseph." Nathanael said to him, "Can any good thing come out of Nazareth?" Philip said to him, "Come and see." Jesus saw Nathanael coming to Him, and said of him, "Behold, an Israelite indeed, in whom there is no deceit!" Nathanael said to Him, "How do You know me?" Jesus answered and said to him, "Before Philip called you, when you were under the fig tree, I saw you." Nathanael answered Him, "Rabbi, You are the Son of God; You are the King of Israel." Jesus answered and said to him, "Because I said to you that I saw you under the fig tree, do you believe? You will see greater things than these".

The appeal to ignorance came from Nathanael when he asked, "Can any good thing come out of Nazareth?" According to Kruse, "Nazareth was such an insignificant place, and one that appears in none of the prophecies concerning the Messiah; so, Nathanael was not willing to accept Philip's testimony."[150] Edwin Blum writes, "Nathanael knew of the poor reputation

---

150 Colin G. Kruse, *John: An Introduction and Commentary*, Tyndale *New Testament Commentaries*, vol. 4 (Downers Grove: InterVarsity Press, 2003), 88.

of Nazareth. Surely the Messiah would come from Jerusalem, Hebron, or some other prominent city."[151] Nathanael was making an argument from an appeal to ignorance. In response, Philip took Nathaniel to Jesus, and once he had encountered Jesus for himself, he rethought his statement and opened his mind to the truth of who Jesus was.

A personal experience with this type of argument occurred during a street witnessing event when sharing with a lost person the following truth claim about God's final judgment: "Only those who have committed their lives to Christ will enter heaven, and the rest God will judge and cast into outer darkness where there will be weeping and gnashing of teeth." In response, the lost person presented the following appeal to ignorance argument: "Isn't it unfair of God to condemn people to hell who have never had the opportunity to hear about Jesus?"

> Premise 1: God is going to condemn to hell those who have never committed their lives to Christ.
>
> Premise 2: Some of those people may have never had the opportunity to hear about Jesus.
>
> Conclusion: Therefore, it would be unfair of God to judge them.

151   Edwin A. Blum, *John, The Bible Knowledge Commentary: An Exposition of the Scriptures*, eds. J. F. Walvoord and R. B. Zuck, vol. 2 (Wheaton: Victor Books, 1985), 276.

The questions asked of the arguer were, "How did you come to the conclusion that God's judgment is unfair, and how do you know that the ones He condemns have never heard?" The error in the argument is the questioning of God's fairness. The arguer was asked a follow-on question, "By what standard are you judging God's fairness? Since God is the standard of justice, no one will be treated unfairly in the final judgment."

The arguer responded with the following statement: "Show me the evidence that can prove my claim wrong." Now came the opportunity to share the following biblical truth:

> Christians have the principle of God's character and His intentions as evidence for His fairness in judgment. Regarding God's character, among God's essential attributes are justice (intense opposition to evil) and grace (passionate love for people). Regarding His intentions, a deep divine passion is to rescue all people. We can reasonably infer, given God's commitment to overcome evil, his longing that all people love him, and his infinite resourcefulness, that his plan is fair.[152]

It could have also been pointed out to the arguer, "Why are you so focused on those who have not heard? It appears from

152 Statement came from the following source: David K. Clark, "Religious Pluralism and Christian Exclusivism," in *To Everyone An Answer: A Case for the Christian Worldview* (Downers Grove: IVP Academic, 2004), 299–300.

your argument that you at least believe in God and that He will judge people based on their acceptance of the gospel. Since you have heard, how are you going to respond?"

Argument from Silence

An argument from silence attempts to demonstrate something as true in the absence of evidence or, more specifically, because of the lack of evidence. It is similar to the appeal to ignorance in that it treats the absence of evidence as evidence itself. For example, Bart Ehrman holds the view that Mark rejected the virgin birth and the higher Christology associated with it because Mark doesn't mention it in his gospel. Ehrman states:

> [Jesus] was already adopted to be God's Son at the very outset of his ministry, when John the Baptist baptized him. This appears to be the view of the Gospel of Mark, in which there is no word of Jesus's pre-existence or of his birth to a virgin. Surely, if this author believed in either view, he would have mentioned it.[153]

This is a clear illustration of the argument from silence. Ehrman assumes that if the writers of the New Testament did

---

153 Bart Ehrman, *How Jesus Became God—The Exaltation of a Jewish Preacher from Galilee* (New York: HarperOne, 2015), 238.

not mention something about Jesus or His teachings, then they must not have believed it. The argument goes as follows:

Premise 1: Mark does not mention the pre-existence of Christ in his gospel.

Premise 2: Mark does not mention the virgin birth of Christ in his gospel.

Conclusion: Therefore, Mark does not believe in the pre-existence or the virgin birth of Christ.

One thing that every Christian must deal with is the issue that Scripture doesn't record everything exhaustively. It doesn't say all that we'd like or hope. Some questions are left unasked and unanswered. Much of what was said or done is simply not recorded in Scripture.

A personal experience with this type of argument occurred during our live radio broadcast from a local restaurant when the following truth claim was made: "Homosexuality is a sinful activity." In response, a listener presented an argument from silence that is heard quite often in our society today, "How can you claim that homosexuality is a sin when Jesus never spoke on the issue?"

Premise 1: Jesus never spoke against homosexuality.

Conclusion: Therefore, you cannot claim that homosexuality is a sin.

The best approach to formulating a response to an argument from silence, such as the one above, is to ask questions. For example, the arguer was asked, "Jesus never mentioned the use of pornography, so is it okay? He never mentioned pedophilia, so is that okay? Jesus never mentioned rape, so is that okay?" Obviously, the answers to these questions are no. At this point, the arguer was shown the truth of what Jesus did mention about human sexuality and how that homosexuality goes against God's created purpose for man and woman. He was read Matthew 19:3–6:

> Some Pharisees came to Jesus, testing Him and asking, "Is it lawful for a man to divorce his wife for any reason at all?" And He answered and said, "Have you not read that He who created them from the beginning made them male and female, and said, 'For this reason a man shall leave his father and mother and be joined to his wife, and the two shall become one flesh'? So they are no longer two, but one flesh. What therefore God has joined together, let no man separate."

It could have also been shared with the arguer the fact that Jesus played a role in the destruction of Sodom and Gomorrah for their indulgence into sexual sin, especially homosexuality.

This is where the arguer might possibly inject a second fallacious argument, a red herring, to move the Christian away from the discussion at hand. He might claim that the destruction was not due to homosexuality but inhospitality, pride, or even rape. The red herring will be discussed in a later chapter.

Finally, the Christian could point out that Jesus did speak out against homosexuality because He and the Father are one. If the arguer believes that Jesus doesn't condemn homosexuality because He never mentions it in His earthly ministry, then he has a great theological problem. The arguer's position would indicate that Jesus and the Father are not in agreement about the issue, which is an impossibility.

The Christian might also share with the arguer what Jesus said in Matthew 15:19–20, "For out of the heart come evil thoughts, murders, adulteries, fornications, thefts, false witness, slanders. These are the things which defile the man." He could explain that the word used for "fornication" is *porneia* and carries the meaning of "illicit sexual intercourse, adultery, fornication, homosexuality, lesbianism, intercourse with animals, etc."[154] Jesus speaks of homosexuality as defiling a man. So Jesus does speak against homosexuality; you just have to understand the meaning of the words being used in Scripture. In using an approach such as this, the Christian has not only

---

154 Strong, *Enhanced Strong's Lexicon.*

responded in a positive way to the argument from silence, but he did so with gentleness and reverence and, in the process, may have created an opportunity for sharing the gospel.

Chapter 10

CRITICAL THINKING AND THE SLIPPERY SLOPE FALLACY

The slippery slope is probably the most well-known and easiest to identify, the logical fallacy. According to Virkler: "Someone commits the fallacy of the slippery slope when he or she claims that we must not take a certain position, not based on facts that can be shown, but because taking that position will put us on a slippery slope that will lead to destructive ends."[155] McDurmon writes that the main idea imagined by the one making the slippery slope argument is "…that a person who takes a first step onto a steep slope will slide all the way to the bottom. Therefore, it argues, it is better to avoid the first step altogether."[156]

McDurmon also states that "Some writers call this the 'domino fallacy' because it assumes taking the first step will cause a chain reaction, and all the dominos will fall to the end of the line."[157]

---

155 Virkler, *Christian's Guide,* 221.
156 McDurmon, *Biblical Logic,* 357.
157 McDurmon, *Biblical Logic,* 357.

An example of a slippery slope argument is found in John 11:47–50:

> Therefore the chief priests and the Pharisees convened a council, and were saying, "What are we doing? For this man is performing many signs. If we let Him go on like this, all men will believe in Him, and the Romans will come and take away both our place and our nation." But one of them, Caiaphas, who was high priest that year, said to them, "You know nothing at all, nor do you take into account that it is expedient for you that one man die for the people, and that the whole nation not perish...".

The slippery slope is found in verse 48. The priests and Pharisees were saying that if they let Jesus continue performing signs and drawing crowds, then the Romans would come and take away their place of power and their nation. Caiaphas was saying that if Jesus didn't die, the whole nation would.

Premise 1: Jesus is performing many signs and drawing large crowds.

Premise 2: If He continues, the Romans will come and take away our place of power and nation.

Conclusion: Therefore, Jesus must not be allowed to continue.

Notice how the conclusion is drawn from the slippery slope in premise 2.

In responding to a slippery slope argument, the Christian should first ask the arguer for his justification in making such a statement. Ask him to provide evidence for his belief. In other words, how he came to his conclusion. In asking him to justify the reasons behind his belief that one event will inevitably go down the slippery slope to another, the Christian might cause him to see the error in his logic and rethink his argument.

The second thing a Christian could do in response to a slippery slope argument is highlight the missing pieces. Highlight the events that are missing from the slope. In emphasizing the possible key events that may occur between the start of the slope and the end, the Christian will be able to demonstrate to the arguer that his argument rests on very shaky ground. For example, in the argument presented from John's gospel, some of the key events that might have to occur before the whole nation dies would be: the numbers of Roman troops in Israel would have to increase; a large number of cities would have to be conquered, and an enormous amount of people would have to die before the nation would be destroyed.

Third, the Christian could use a slippery slope example of his own. This approach would involve attacking the arguer's slippery slope with one of his own, preferably one centered around the topic they are discussing. To illustrate, go back to the slippery slope argument from John's gospel; the Christian's example could be, "If we let Jesus go on like this, the Romans may come to believe in Him and then they would force us to believe." The Christian's example would demonstrate the absurdity of the slippery slope argument used by the arguer and possibly cause him to rethink his position.

A personal experience with this type of argument occurred during a walk through the mall at Christmas time, and a lost person overheard a conversation this writer had with his wife concerning the displaying of nativity scenes in public, "Nativity scenes are so beautiful, and they communicate the message of the birth of our Savior. I just can't understand why they cannot be displayed in public places." In response, the lost person presented the following slippery slope argument, "Allowing a nativity scene in a public space is the first step toward a theocratic state with someone like Pat Robertson making all the rules."

The flow of the argument is as follows:

Premise 1: Allowing a nativity scene in a public space is the first step toward a theocratic state.

Premise 2: A theocratic state would allow someone like Pat Robertson to make all the rules.

Conclusion: Therefore, nativity scenes should not be allowed to be displayed in a public space.

The arguer's conclusion is drawn from the slippery slope in premise 1. In response, the arguer was asked how he came to that conclusion. After listening to his answer, this writer highlighted some possible events that were missing from the slippery slope. In this argument, one event that was pointed out to the arguer was that of elections—elections determine the leaders in our nation, so for Pat Robertson or any other theologian to be placed in a position where they would be able to make all the decisions for our nation, they would have to be elected by the people. Third, this writer provided a slippery slope of his own—removing nativity scenes from public spaces is the first step toward the removal of all Christmas decorations in any place where the public gathers. Any decoration resembling the true reason for the celebration of Christmas would have to be removed. For example, the candy cane, the star at the top of the Christmas tree, Christmas lights, etc.

The goal for understanding the slippery slope fallacy is to be able to respond to the argument in such a way that the arguer sees the weakness of his position and possibly opens the door for sharing the gospel. In the scenario presented above, the arguer did see the error in his statement, and this writer did have the opportunity to share with him the meanings of many of the decorations used to celebrate Christmas. He did not, however, accept the gospel message when presented, but the seed had been planted.

Chapter 11

CRITICAL THINKING AND THE FALSE DILEMMA FALLACY

———

A false dilemma, or sometimes called false dichotomy, is a type of informal fallacy in which something is falsely claimed to be an "either/or" situation, when in fact, there is at least one additional option. Take, for example, Matthew 22:15–22:

> Then the Pharisees went and plotted together how they might trap Him in what He said. And they sent their disciples to Him, along with the Herodians, saying, "Teacher, we know that You are truthful and teach the way of God in truth, and defer to no one; for You are not partial to any. Tell us then, what do You think? Is it lawful to give a poll-tax to Caesar, or not?" But Jesus perceived their malice, and said, "Why are you testing Me, you hypocrites? Show Me the coin used for the poll-tax." And they brought Him a denarius. And He said to them, "Whose likeness and inscription is this?" They said to Him, "Caesar's." Then He said to them, "Then render to Caesar the things that are Caesar's; and to God the things that are God's." And hearing this, they were

amazed, and leaving Him, they went away.

The argument can be diagrammed as follows:

Premise 1: You are truthful and teach the way of God in truth.

Premise 2: You are not partial to anyone.

Conclusion: Therefore, is it lawful to give a poll tax to Caesar or not?

The Pharisees were constant in their attempts to trap Jesus. They plotted and schemed to come up with arguments that would make Him look foolish in front of His followers. In the example above, the Pharisees are using a false dichotomy to entrap Him. In verse 15, Matthew tells us that the Pharisees came together for the purpose of devising a scheme that would accomplish their goal. The false dilemma they developed and presented to Jesus was whether or not it was proper for the Jews to pay taxes to Caesar. As Barney Kasdan explains:

If he responded positively, then the *P'rushim* would have had a major accusation against Yeshua as one who placed the pagan empire above. have verifiable evidence of one who advocates political rebellion. They thought they had this self-proclaimed Messiah painted into a corner with no viable way out.[158]

However, they never anticipated Jesus's response. Jesus presented a third alternative in verse 21, "...render to Caesar the things that are Caesar's; and to God the things that are God's." His response left His opponents speechless.

Through the false dilemma presented by the Pharisees, Jesus provided Christians with an example of how to respond to such an argument. Jesus's use of critical thinking, logic had the effect of silencing His detractors while, at the same time, communicating truth. This is an example Christians should follow. To counter a false dilemma, the best approach is to show that there are additional options beyond the ones that are being presented.

An example of a false dilemma is found in a March 5, 2019, article by Beatrice Alba titled "If we reject gender discrimination in every other arena, why do we accept it in religion?"[159] In her opening paragraph, she writes, "The church's exclusion of women from the priesthood and the sexist notions embedded in religious dogma violate our 21st-century princi-

158 Barney Kasdan, *Matthew Presents Yeshua King Messiah: A Messianic Commentary* (Clarksville: Messianic Jewish Publishers, 2011), 251.
159 Beatrice Alba, "If we reject gender discrimination in every other arena, why do we accept it in religion?" *The Guardian*, March 5, 2019, https://www.theguardian.com/commentisfree/2019/mar/06/if-we-reject-gender-discrimination-in-every-other-arena-why-do-we-accept-it-in-religion.

ples of equality and social justice." She then presents her false dilemma:

> Yet religion is seen as sacred, and we find ourselves walking on eggshells around the topic. But as long as religions disrespect and marginalize almost half of the population, they should not be immune to criticism. We need to ask ourselves what is really sacred: respecting the traditions of a bygone era, or basic principles of social justice. If religions get it so wrong on this basic issue of social justice and human rights, why would we owe them any deference?

Premise 1: As long as religions disrespect and marginalize almost half of the population, they should not be immune to criticism.

Premise 2: The choice is between respecting traditions of a bygone era or basic principles of social justice.

Conclusion: So if religions get it so wrong on this basic issue of social justice and human rights, why would we owe them any deference?

Alba's false dilemma is: What is really sacred, respecting the traditions of a bygone era or the basic principles of social justice? She is offering two options in determining the role of women in the ministry: old traditions or social justice. Questions the Christian could ask her are: "What do you mean by 'traditions of a bygone era'?" and "What do you mean by 'social justice'?" Then point her to the third alternative, "biblical authority," and share the appropriate passages of Scripture (1 Timothy 2:12, 3:2; Titus 1:6). Her answers to the two questions will demonstrate that her argument is not resting on the one and only true authority for church order and governance. By responding in this manner, the Christian has not only refuted her argument but has possibly opened the door for sharing more biblical truth.

A personal experience with this type of argument occurred during a street witnessing event when discussing the issue of the biblical account of creation with a lost person. The false dilemma presented by the individual was as follows: "I am a student of science, and if you accept the biblical account of creation, you are rejecting science."

Premise 1: I am a student of science.

Premise 2: If you accept the biblical account of creation, you are rejecting science.

Conclusion: Therefore, you cannot believe in creation and science.

The two alternatives being presented by the arguer are—you

are either a believer in creation or a believer in science. Those are the only two options. The arguer was asked, "Have you ever given any thought to the fact that there are many modern-day scientists who are also creationists? A search of the internet will provide you with the names of these scientists and their fields of expertise." With the use of a smartphone, internet access was gained, and a list was shown to the arguer. By responding in this manner, the arguer was shown the error of his statement, and the door was opened for sharing gospel.

An argument similar to this one was raised by Sam Harris in a discussion centered around faith and science. He states, "We have people like Francis Collins[160] who think that on Sunday you can kneel down in the dewy grass and give yourself to Jesus because you're in the presence of a frozen waterfall, and on Monday you can be a physical geneticist."[161] Harris is attempting to show that one cannot bow down and worship God because of the magnificence of His creation on one day and then on the next, serve as a scientist. He is presenting a false dilemma much like the one above. The response of the Christian would be to ask the questions, "Can you explain what you

160 Francis Sellers Collins is an American physician-geneticist who discovered the genes associated with a number of diseases and led the Human Genome Project. Collins has written a number of books on science, medicine, and religion, including the *New York Times* bestseller, *The Language of God: A Scientist Presents Evidence for Belief.*
161 Hitchens, Dawkins, Harris, and Dennett, *The Four Horsemen*, 88.

mean by that statement? How did you come to the conclusion that you cannot be a faithful Christian and at the same time be a scientist?" After his response, the Christian could then present him with a list of modern-day scientists who are also devout Christians. This type of response can show the arguer the error of his statement and possibly open the door for sharing the gospel.

Chapter 12

CRITICAL THINKING AND THE
APPEAL TO FEAR OR FORCE FALLACY

———

This type of fallacy is one that, as noted in its name, plays upon people's fear. In particular, this fallacy presents a scary future if a certain decision is made today. For example, a mother tells her children not to leave the yard because there could be wild animals in the woods. Or a politician stating that if we don't switch to alternate forms of energy, we will destroy the earth.

An example found in the Bible comes from John 19:10. When Pilate could not get an answer from Jesus, he tried to pressure Him with fear, "You do not speak to me? Do you not know that I have authority to release You, and I have authority to crucify You?"

Premise 1: Where are You from? (John 19:9)

Premise 2: You do not speak to me?

Conclusion: Do you not know that I have authority to release You, and I have authority to crucify You?

Jesus provides His response in verse 11, "Jesus answered, 'You would have no authority over Me, unless it had been given you from above; for this reason, he who delivered Me to you has the greater sin.'" Whether or not Pilate fulfills his threat does not change the truth of who Jesus is or where He comes from. That is the point that must be kept in mind when faced with the appeal to fear fallacy; it has no impact on the truth.

A personal experience with this type of argument occurred during a live radio broadcast from a local restaurant when the following truth claim was made: "Abortion is a profoundly immoral and unjust act. The taking of an innocent human life when it is most defenseless. As Christians committed to justice and righteousness, we cannot stand by and just let that happen. Abortion needs to be outlawed." In response, a listener presented the following appeal to fear argument: "Outlawing abortion would just force women into the back alleys, and they could die. Do you want women to die because they couldn't get the health care they needed because it has been outlawed?"

Premise 1: Outlawing abortion would just force women into the back alleys.

Premise 2: Women could die.

Conclusion: Therefore, "Do you want women to die because they couldn't get the health care they needed because it has been outlawed?"

The best approach for the Christian is to meet the appeal to fear head-on. Let the arguer know that his argument is one designed to frighten believers in the hope that they will change their opinion, but it will not impact his faith or the truthfulness of the gospel. In this case, the argument does not change the truth that abortion is the killing of an unborn infant—it is the taking of an innocent human life. Standing firm in the face of an appeal to fear will allow the Christian to demonstrate to the arguer the reality of his faith and may possibly create an opportunity for sharing the gospel.

This is one of those fallacies where it might be difficult to respond in a way that will show the error of the argument and create an opportunity for sharing the gospel. There have been Christians who have been faced with an appeal to fear, either recant your faith or lose your life. Many have chosen to suffer the consequences of refusing to yield to the fallacy. They lost their life, their freedom, their job, their family, but it did not change the truth of their message or their faith. As a Christian in the United States, you won't, at least in this day and time, have to face the loss of your life for your faith or belief in the truthfulness of the Bible, but you might have to face the possibility of the loss of a job or career. You may even have to face the possibility of the loss of friends or family. Or, as we have seen under the "stay at home order" during the coronavirus, face being arrested or fined while sitting in your car for attending a drive-in church service. How will you respond? As the Apostle Paul encourages believers in 1 Corinthians 16:13, "Be on the alert, stand firm in the faith, act like men, be strong."

Chapter 13

CRITICAL THINKING AND THE APPEAL TO PITY FALLACY

This fallacy defies logic as it attempts to distract from the truth of the conclusion by the use of pity. People use this fallacy whenever they try to use human sympathy rather than facts to move a person or group of people toward a conclusion. For example, a man is pulled over for speeding, and the officer gives him a fine for speeding. The man argues with the officer about whether he was speeding or not, then realizes he isn't going to win the argument. So he resorts to telling the officer that he was speeding to the hospital because his wife was having a baby, and he wanted to make sure he witnessed his child's birth. Whether this is true or not is irrelevant to the fact that he was speeding. He attempted to get the officer to have pity on him to get him past the fact that he was breaking the law.

An appeal to pity is used to distract people in arguments for the purpose of appealing to their emotions. Playing on the pity that someone feels for an individual or group can certainly affect what that person thinks about the group; this is a highly effective and quite common fallacy. However, this type of argument is fallacious because our emotional responses are not really a good guide to truth; emotions can cloud rather than clarify issues. One problem of using an emotional response as a justification for an action is that once the emotion wears off, so does the rationale for taking that action, even if nothing has changed.

In Matthew 25:14–30, Jesus presents the "Parable of the Talents." A rich man is about to go on a journey, so he decides to entrust his possessions to his slaves. To one slave, he gave five talents, to another two, and to another one. While he was away, the one with the five talents made investments and doubled them. The one with two talents did the same. The slave who had the one talent buried it in the ground. When the rich man returned from his journey, he called in his slaves to give an accounting on how they handled his possessions. Two of the slaves were able to show the man that they had doubled the amount he had given them, and in return, they were appropriately rewarded.

However, the one who was given just a single talent was a different story. Kasdan explains:

Although he had received only one talent, one would expect him to have at least matched the amount given him but he did not do so. He starts his explanation on shaky ground, as

144

he addresses the master as *a hard man*. In addition to this negative salutation, the servant continues by denigrating the master as one who would *harvest where he didn't plant and gather where he didn't sow seed.* Because of these perceptions, the final servant admits that he *was afraid* of the owner, so much so that he hid his *talent in the ground.* With an obvious attitude, this servant offers to give his talent back to the owner, with no profit or labor to show for it.[162]

Premise 1: You are a hard man.

Premise 2: I was afraid, so I hid your talent in the ground.

Conclusion: So please forgive me.[163]

In his response to his master, the slave uses an appeal to pity as his explanation for why he did not use the one talent to make a profit. Notice he says his master was a "hard man," and he was "afraid" of him, and that is why he hid the talent in the ground. The man did not buy into the slave's appeal to pity

162 Kasdan, *Matthew Presents Yeshua*, 319.
163 In this example from Scripture, there is a missing conclusion to the argument being presented by the slave. In a case such as this, the reader will need to determine what the missing conclusion might be. To determine what the missing conclusion might possibly be, look at context of the statement and ask yourself the following questions: "Does the information provided in the statement propose a conclusion that is unstated? What is the statement attempting to convince me of? What is it trying to get me to believe, do, or endorse?" In this example, the slave is seeking forgiveness for not investing the one talent given to him.

and punished him appropriately. He did not let his emotions control his actions.

We can see a different response and outcome to an appeal to pity in the parable of a king deciding to settle accounts with his slaves as recorded in Matthew 18:23–34. In this parable, a king began calling in his slaves to demand payment of money owed to him. One slave owed such a large amount that it would be impossible to pay, so the king ordered that he and his whole family be sold into slavery until the debt was paid in full. The slave fell down before the king, pleading with him to have patience, and he would repay him everything. This was his appeal to pity, and the king, moved with compassion, released him and forgave him the total debt. Happy ending? No! This is a good example of why we should not allow emotions to control our responses. As stated earlier, emotions can cloud rather than clarify issues.

Premise 1: The slave did not have the means to repay the debt.

Premise 2: His wife and children were ordered to be sold into slavery to cover the debt.

Conclusion: In response, the slave fell to the ground and begged for forgiveness.

You would have expected that the slave would have been very grateful to the king and would have displayed that gratefulness in how he treated others. But in reading the rest of the parable, it is discovered that shortly after being set free by the king, this slave encounters a fellow slave who owed him a very small amount of money. He demanded that his fellow slave immediately pay him what he owed. The fellow slave begged him to have patience, and he would pay him what he owed. He, too, used an appeal to pity. However, the slave who had been forgiven such a large debt refused to allow this man's appeal to pity to affect the outcome. He had the man thrown in prison until he could repay all that was owed to him.

Premise 1: A fellow slave owed the forgiven slave a small amount of money.

Premise 2: The fellow slave could not pay what he owed.

Conclusion: So the fellow slave begged for forgiveness.

In the first parable, the rich man did not allow his emotions to dictate his response. Instead, his response was in accordance with the laws/customs of the culture. The king in the second parable, however, allowed his emotions to dictate his response, and the results had a negative impact on another individual.

The question before the Christian, then, is: How does he

prevent emotions from dictating his response to an appeal to pity? By asking questions that will enable him to discover the truth behind the appeal to pity. By asking the right questions, the king in the second parable may have had discovered that the heart of the slave making the appeal was not sincere and truthful.

Today, the appeal to pity usually arises when debating social issues, like abortion, same-sex marriage, etc. On the abortion issue, the Christian might hear something like, "Some women are too poor to raise a child. Therefore, abortion should be legal." If Christians allow emotions to dictate their responses, they might possibly choose to agree.

But how does it follow that because someone is too poor to raise a child, she may kill the child? In response to such an appeal to pity, the Christian could ask the question, "Would it be permissible for a woman to kill her two-year-old child because of poverty?" Of course not. So why would we justify abortion for the same reason? The truth is the life in the womb is just as valuable as the life outside the womb.

Sam Harris offers an appeal to pity argument in a discussion over the Christian's stand against embryonic stem cell research. According to Harris, "The problem with this research, from the religious point of view, is simple: it entails the destruction of human embryos."[164] He further adds:

> Their concern is not merely that a collection of 150 cells
> may suffer its destruction. Rather, they believe that even
> a human zygote (a fertilized egg) should be accorded all
> the protections of a fully developed human being. Such a
> cell, after all, has the potential to become a fully developed
> human being.[165]

Harris's appeal to pity is as follows:

> There is not the slightest reason to believe, however, that
> such embryos have the capacity to sense pain, to suffer, or
> to experience the loss of life in any way at all. What is in-
> disputable is there are millions of human beings who do
> have these capacities, and who currently suffer from trau-
> matic injuries to the brain and spinal cord. Millions more
> suffer from Parkinson's and Alzheimer's diseases. Millions
> more suffer from stroke and heart disease, from burns, from
> diabetes, from rheumatoid arthritis, from Purkinje cell de-
> generation, from Duchenne muscular dystrophy, and from
> vision and hearing loss. We know that embryonic stem cells
> promise to be a renewable source of tissues and organs that
> might alleviate such suffering in the not-too-distant fu-
> ture.[166]

164 Harris, *The End of Faith*, 165.
165 Harris, *The End of Faith*, 166.
166 Harris, *The End of Faith*, 166.

Premise 1: Embryos do not have the capacity to sense pain, to suffer, or to experience the loss of life in any way at all.

Premise 2: Millions of people are suffering from traumatic injuries and debilitating diseases for which embryonic stem cells might alleviate.

Conclusion: Therefore, Christians should change their minds about objecting to embryonic stem cell research in order to help eliminate such suffering.[167]

Harris's intent in his appeal to pity is to use the examples of people who are suffering from severe injuries and devastating diseases to play on the sympathies of those who stand against embryonic stem cell research. This research could find a way of eliminating the pain and suffering people are now having to endure, and the Christian is preventing it from happening.

A personal experience with this type of argument occurred during a live radio broadcast from a local restaurant when the following truth claim was made: "Same-sex marriage should not be allowed, for the Bible states that marriage is to be between one man and one woman for life—Genesis 2:24, 'For

167 This is another example of an argument that does not have a conclusion, and it is up to the listener/reader to provide one. In the case of Harris's argument, the best way to determine the missing conclusion is to search for a way of completing the argument that (1) is a plausible way of interpreting the arguer's intent and (2) makes the argument as good an argument as it can be. This can be accomplished with Harris's argument by reading the complete section, *The God of Medicine*, pages 165–169.

this reason a man shall leave his father and his mother, and be joined to his wife; and they shall become one flesh.'" In response, a listener presented the following appeal to pity argument: "Marriage is a basic human right, and I think denying people that right is unloving and just plain wrong. How could you even consider denying marriage to two people who love each other?"

Premise 1: Marriage is a basic human right.

Premise 2: Denying people that right is unloving and just plain wrong.

Conclusion: Therefore, you should be supportive of same-sex marriage.

The appeal to pity in this argument is a very strong one. To prevent emotions from dictating his response, the Christian should begin by asking questions that will enable him to discover the truth behind the appeal; in other words, what is the reason the arguer is making such an appeal. In the example above, the arguer may be taking such a position because he has a friend or family member who is involved in a same-sex marriage. By asking questions such as, "What do you mean by that statement?" and "How did you come to that conclusion?" can help the believer discover the reason behind the appeal to pity. This information can help him develop a response that is gentle and compassionate and possibly create an opportunity for sharing the gospel.

The Christian's response to an appeal to pity should be one that is comprised of both compassion and reasonableness. There are several approaches the Christian can choose from in response to such an argument:

1. Point out the logical flaw in the argument. This involves explaining why the arguer's argument is fallacious and pointing out his lack of evidence or his use of unsound reasoning.

2. Point out the attempted manipulation. This involves pointing out the fact that the arguer is attempting to manipulate the Christian's emotions and explaining how exactly the arguer is trying to do it.

3. Address their emotional argument with facts. This involves using facts in order to try and negate the emotional effect that the arguer is attempting to create, for example, by proving that the basis of his argument is wrong.

4. Stick to the original line of reasoning. Sometimes the best course of action is to simply ignore the arguer's appeal to pity and stick to the original argument being presented.

In responding to the argument concerning same-sex marriage, the third response would be the best. The Christian could ask, "Would you allow any two people who love one another to get married? What about a father and daughter or mother and son? Or would you allow a thirty-year-old man marry a ten-year-old girl if they loved one another?" This would illustrate to the one making the argument that the basis of his position for marriage, just being in love, is wrong. The Christian can now share the biblical basis for marriage.

In Harris's appeal to pity, the third approach would be the best as well. The Christian could ask, "Did you know that stem cell research can be done without the destruction of a human embryo? What about umbilical cord stem cells? Did you know that a baby's umbilical cord is made up of tissue and contains blood? Both cord blood and cord tissue are rich sources of powerful stem cells. Cord blood stem cells are currently used in transplant medicine to regenerate healthy blood and immune systems. These cells are being researched for their ability to act like our body's own personal repair kit and may be able to help our bodies heal in new ways." Questions such as these can help illustrate to the arguer the error in his statement. The Christian can now share, from Scripture, his reasons for opposing embryonic stem cell research. For example, Christians oppose embryonic stem cell research because there is no way, at least today, to take stem cells from human embryos, pre-born children, without killing them. According to Scripture, all men are created in the image of God, and it begins the moment of conception.

> Genesis 1:27, "God created man in His own image, in the image of God He created him; male and female He created them."

> Jeremiah 1:5, "Before I formed you in the womb I knew you, And before you were born I consecrated you; I have appointed you a prophet to the nations."

> Psalm 139:16, "Your eyes have seen my unformed substance; And in Your book were all written the days that were ordained for me, when as yet there was not one of them."

Whichever of the four approaches the Christian chooses, it should not only demonstrate the flaw in the arguer's use of the appeal to pity but also possibly create an opportunity for sharing the gospel.

Chapter 14

CRITICAL THINKING AND THE RED HERRING FALLACY

In a red herring fallacy, the arguer attempts to divert attention away from the issue at hand by pointing to an unrelated yet strongly compelling line of thought. This tactic will attempt to get you to follow the new subject while neglecting to press for an answer to the original argument.

The red herring gets its name from a technique used to train hunting dogs. In the evening, the dog trainer will take the body of a dead animal (rabbit, squirrel, etc.) and drag it through the training ground. Through the evening, the trail will grow cold. The next morning the trainer drags a smoked red herring tied to a string diagonally across the path he had made the former evening. He then lets the dog in training out on the original trail. When the dog gets to the point where the path of the red herring crosses the older trail, he will usually be distracted by the fresher, stronger scent of the red herring. The trainer then pulls him back and puts him on the original trail, helping him learn to stay on that trail.

McDurmon provides an example of a red herring: "Atheists and critics of the faith employ many diversion tactics amidst their arguments. You will often hear something like this: 'Christian faith doesn't improve morality. Just look at the Crusades! That kind of slaughter exposes Christianity for the tyranny that it really is.[168]'" The red herring employed by the atheists is the statement, "Christian faith doesn't improve morality. Just look at the Crusades!"

McDurmon's response:

> The behavior of some professing Christians does not establish or disestablish, and thus is irrelevant to, the truth or efficacy of the Christian faith itself. Even if the vast majority of Christians at a given time in history turned warlike and bloodthirsty (this has never been the case—even during the Crusades), this would still not discredit the faith itself. It would more likely exemplify a departure from Christian morals, and thus cry out the need for more Christian faith.[169]

Notice in McDurmon's response he did not take the bait, the red herring, and enter into a debate about the evils of the Crusades. He stayed on point—the Christian faith.

A biblical example of a red herring comes from the story of Jesus's encounter with the Samaritan woman at the well (John

---

168 McDurmon, *Biblical Logic*, 326.
169 McDurmon, *Biblical Logic,* 326.

4:7–26). The story begins with Jesus asking the woman for a drink of water. She was stunned by His request because Jews had no dealings with the Samaritans. Jesus then tells her in verse 10, "If you knew the gift of God, and who it is who says to you, 'Give Me a drink,' you would have asked Him, and He would have given you living water." Jesus explains to her that whoever drinks this water will never thirst again, and so she asks Him to give her that water so she will not have to come to the well again. Jesus then asks her to go call her husband, to which she responds she has no husband. In verses 17–18, Jesus said to her, "You have correctly said, 'I have no husband'; for you have had five husbands, and the one whom you now have is not your husband; this you have said truly." In verses 19–20, the woman pulls out a red herring, for she says, "Sir, I perceive that You are a prophet. Our fathers worshiped in this mountain, and you people say that in Jerusalem is the place where men ought to worship." She is attempting to divert attention from the issue being raised, her life situation, by pointing to an unrelated yet strongly compelling line of thought, the true place of worship. She wanted Jesus to follow the new topic instead of pressing for an answer to the question about her life situation.

Premise 1: I perceive that You are a prophet.
Premise 2: Our fathers worshipped in this mountain.

Premise 3: You people say that Jerusalem is the place where men ought to worship.

Conclusion: So tell me where the true place of worship is.

It is understandable that she would want to change the subject because her life situation was not one to brag about. She had been married five times and was currently living with someone who was not her husband. According to Gerald Borchert, her life was one of sexual immorality. He writes, "After experimenting with five husbands (which should not be allegorized), she no longer found the marriage ritual necessary."[170] Colin Kruse explains her situation this way:

The word translated "husband" (*anēr*) in the NIV can mean either "husband" or "man" (a male). If we take *anēr* to mean "husband" she could have been married five times and each time her husband had died, or each time she had been divorced (in a society where divorce was almost entirely a male prerogative), and now she was living with a man who was not her husband (meaning someone else's husband). If *anēr* is taken to mean "a man," it is possible that she had never been married, but had had a series of affairs with men, culminating in a final adulterous relationship. The text does

170   Gerald L. Borchert, John 1–11, *The New American Commentary*, vol. 25A (Nashville: Broadman & Holman Publishers, 1996), 205–06.

not enable us to determine which of these interpretations is correct. Either way, it seems Jesus' intention in mentioning these things was not to create a sense of guilt, but to confront the pain in her relationships with men. This would accentuate her thirst for a meaningful relationship with God and make her receptive to the revelation he was offering her.[171]

Eli Lizorkin-Eyzenberg describes her situation as follows:

The mere fact of having had multiple husbands is not a sin in and of itself. In ancient Israelite society, women did not initiate a divorce. Her five husbands could have died of sickness, been killed by bandits, perished in battle, or simply divorced her because of infertility. Still, in any of these cases, the result would have been devastating to her each time. Jesus stated that she was currently living with a man who was not her husband.

Many assume this meant that the woman was cohabitating with her boyfriend. However, this is not explicitly stated. Because she would need some means of support, she may have lived with a distant relative or in some other undesirable arrangement in order to survive. In her Aramaic speaking culture, it was important for a woman to have a

---

171 Colin G. Kruse, *John: An Introduction and Commentary, Tyndale New Testament* Commentaries, vol. 4 (Downers Grove: InterVarsity Press, 2003), 133–34.

male protector around her at every stage of her life. These protector males, called "gowra" in Aramaic (from a root meaning "strength") could be a male cousin, uncle, or other guardian responsible to take care of her.

Moreover, Samaritan Israelites did not practice Levirate marriage as did Judean and Galilean Israelites (a group to which Jesus belonged). Samaritans believed that the benefit of Levirate marriage should not apply to a woman if her marriage had been consummated. It is likely that Jesus was not nailing her to the cross of justice, but instead was telling her that he knew everything about the pain she had endured. This is certainly more consistent with the Jesus we know from other stories.[172]

A personal experience with this type of argument occurred during a live radio broadcast from a local restaurant when the following truth claim was made: "Biblical truth is objective truth." In response, a listener presented the following red herring argument: "The Bible cannot be an objective guide to truth because so many people disagree on the right interpretation of it, and that's why we have all those different translations."

The red herring in the example above is the statement, "... so many people disagree on the right interpretation of the Bi-

172 Eli Lizorkin-Eyzenberg, "Rethinking the Samaritan Woman," Israel Bible Weekly, accessed April 2, 2020, https://weekly.israelbiblecenter.com/rethinking-samaritan-woman/.

ble, and that's why we have all those different translations."
The arguer is attempting to distract from the truth claim that
Bible truth is objective truth and enter into a debate about the
various translations. The argument outlines as follows:

Premise 1: There are so many disagreements on the right
interpretation of a biblical passage.

Premise 2: We have many different translations of the Bible.

Conclusion: Therefore, the Bible cannot be an objective
guide to truth.

There are four options available for the Christian to choose
from in deciding how to respond to the red herring: (1) He can
continue discussing the original issue and ignore the red herring. (2) He can point out the red herring to his opponent and
its irrelevance to the topic and then continue his discussion. (3)
He can choose to follow the trail of the red herring. Sometimes
this may be the only way to ensure that the discussion continues in a reasonable and productive manner. In the example
above, the Christian could explain that different translations
result from different principles of translation, and even though
there are different translations, they all say the same thing.
He can also point out that there are many ways to communicate the same truth and that different translations can actually

enhance our understanding by phrasing the truth in different ways. The goal of the response is to get the conversation back to the original issue being discussed. (4) The Christian can end the conversation and walk away. It may come to the point that the Christian realizes there is simply no point in carrying the discussion any further since the arguer continues his attempt to divert attention away from the main issue. The Christian should let the arguer know that he is ending the conversation because of his continued use of the red herring and his unwillingness to stay on the issue.

In the chapter describing the "argument from silence" fallacy, a personal experience was provided in which an arguer made the following statement: "How can you claim that homosexuality is a sin when Jesus never spoke on the issue?" When pointing out to the arguer that Jesus did speak out against homosexuality because He played a role in the destruction of Sodom and Gomorrah, the arguer might insert a red herring fallacy by making the claim that the destruction was not due to the sin of homosexuality but was because of inhospitality, pride, or even rape. The arguer is attempting to get the Christian off the subject at hand by offering alternative reasons for the destruction of the two cities. The best approach for the Christian to take is number two: He should point out the red herring to the arguer and its irrelevance to the issue that Jesus never spoke against homosexuality. The Christian can then continue the discussion by pointing out that Jesus and the Father are one, and if the arguer believes that Jesus doesn't condemn homosexuality because He never mentions it in His earthly ministry, then he has a great theological problem. The arguer's position would indicate that Jesus and the Father are not in agreement about the issue, which is an impossibility.

Whichever approach the Christian chooses, he should keep in mind that his response should not only demonstrate the flaw in the arguer's use of the red herring but also possibly create an opportunity for sharing the gospel.

Chapter 15

CRITICAL THINKING AND SELF-REFUTING ARGUMENTS

A self-refuting argument is one that fails to meet its own standard. In other words, it is an argument that cannot live up to its own criteria. For example, if someone were to say, "I cannot speak a word in English," it is obvious that he just did. The statement defeated itself. Recognizing self-refuting arguments is critical for being a clear thinker and a good defender of the faith.

J. P. Moreland has defined three criteria for helping to identify self-refuting arguments: (1) Does the argument establish a requirement of acceptability? (2) Does the argument place itself in subjection to the requirement? And (3) does the argument fall short of satisfying its own requirement?[173] Using the statement "I cannot speak a word in English":

1. Does the argument establish a requirement of acceptability? Yes, what is spoken must be spoken in English.

173

2. Does the argument place itself in subjection to the requirement? Yes, the individual said that he could not speak a word of English.

3. Does the argument fall short of satisfying its own requirement? Yes, what he spoke, he spoke in English, which is what he said he could not do.

How should a Christian respond to self-refuting arguments? By turning the claim back on itself. Using the example, "I cannot speak a word in English," in turning the claim back on itself, you would say, "You just did." Here are some more examples of self-refuting arguments that can be checked against the three criteria presented by Moreland and how a Christian should respond.

"There is no truth": If there is no truth, then this argument is false because there would be at least one truth, namely, that there is no truth. In response, the Christian should ask, "Is that true?"

"You should not judge": This argument is a judgment, so it refutes itself. When someone makes this argument, the Christian should ask, "Then why are you judging me!"

"The scientific method is the only means of knowing truth": If this claim were true, then it would be false since it is a claim to truth that is not known by the scientific method. The

Christian should ask in response to this argument, "Can that be proven scientifically?"

"History is unknowable": If true, then this very argument would be unknowable. Why? By the time the last word of this statement is read, the first two words are already history. Thus, even comprehending this argument implies that at least some things from the past can be known in the present. In response, the Christian could say, "You can't know whether your statement is true or not because by the time you have finished making the statement, it is history."

"You should be tolerant of views not your own": Usually, this argument is made by someone that has just been challenged about the validity of a view they hold. For example, they are challenged about their acceptance of same-sex marriage, and they respond with, "You should be tolerant of views not your own." The Christian's response should be, "Then why are you not tolerant about my view?"

"Language cannot carry meaning": The Christian's response to such a claim should be, "If that is true, then how can I understand what you just said?"

"What's true for you isn't true for me": If so, then this claim is only true for the one who makes it and isn't true for anyone else. Why, then, is the person bothering to make the claim in the first place since he obviously believes it does ap-

ply to others? The Christian's response should be, "Is that true for all people?"

"You should not force your morals on others": In making such an argument, the person, without realizing it, is forcing their morals on you. The Christian's response should be, "Then why are you forcing yours on me?"

"Only stupid people use insults": The Christian's response, "You seem to be insulting me."

"I can't think of anything to say": The Christian's response, "You just did."

"All truth claims are just are just attempts for power and control": The Christian's response, "Is that true for your claim?"

"Doctrine doesn't matter": The Christian's response, "Isn't that a doctrinal statement?"

From these examples, it is obvious why they are called self-refuting arguments. The important thing to remember with self-refuting arguments is that they are necessarily false. In other words, there is no possible way for them to be true. This is because they violate a very fundamental law of logic, the law of non-contradiction. This law states that A and non-A cannot both be true at the same time and in the same sense. For example, either the theists are right—God exists—or the atheists are—God doesn't exist. Both cannot be true.

Chapter 16

CRITICAL THINKING AND TRUTH CLAIMS CONTAINING MORE THAN ONE FALLACY

———

There are times when a believer is going to be confronted with an argument against the Christian worldview in which he will not have an immediate answer and in which he will need time to do research. There is nothing wrong with the Christian asking the arguer for that time and then setting a date to get back together to continue the discussion. It is important to keep the lines of communication open if the believer is going to be successful at pointing out the errors in a fallacious claim raised against the Christian worldview.

There are also times when the Christian will face an argument in which the arguer has used several logical fallacies as evidence in support of his main truth claim. For example, in the following argument, Harris has used an ad hominem, a false dilemma, and an appeal to pity. It is Harris's conviction that the Christian is wrong to believe that there is no universal standard of morality unless the Bible is accepted as the word of God. He states, "We can easily think of objective sources of moral order that do not require the existence of a law-giving God. For there to be objective moral truths worth knowing, there need only be better and worse ways to seek happiness in the world."[174] In defense of his belief, Harris writes:

> One of the most pernicious effects of religion is that it tends to divorce morality from the reality of human suffering. Religion allows people to imagine that their concerns are moral when they are not—that is, when they have nothing to do with suffering or its alleviation. Indeed, religion allows people to imagine their concerns are moral when they are highly immoral—that is when pressing these concerns inflicts unnecessary and appalling suffering on innocent human beings. This explains why Christians like yourself expend more "moral" energy opposing abortion than fighting genocide. It explains why you are more concerned about human embryos than about the lifesaving promise of stem-cell research. And it explains why you can preach against condom use in sub-Saharan Africa while millions die from AIDS there each year.[175]

In the ad hominem portion of his argument, Harris is attacking religion and those associated with it because he believes its moral teachings ignore and contribute to the sufferings of many people. His argument flows as follows:

---

174   Harris, *Letter*, 23.
175   Harris, *Letter*, 25.

Premise 1: Religion allows people to imagine that their concerns are moral when they are not—that is, when they have nothing to do with suffering or its alleviation.

Premise 2: Religion allows people to imagine their concerns are moral when they are highly immoral—that is, when pressing these concerns inflicts unnecessary and appalling suffering on innocent human beings.

Conclusion: Therefore, one of the most pernicious effects of religion is that it tends to divorce morality from the reality of human suffering.

The best response for the Christian is to ask Harris to explain his statement and how he came to that conclusion. Harris attempts to do so by describing how conservative Christians in our government:

> ...have resisted a vaccination program for the human papillomavirus (HPV) on the grounds that HPV is a valuable impediment to premarital sex. These pious men and women want to preserve cervical cancer as an incentive to abstinence, even if it sacrifices the lives of thousands of women each year.[176]

This is an example of a response that may require some

---

176 Harris, *Letter*, 26–7.

research on the part of the Christian in order to refute such a statement. The Christian should ask for time and then set a date to get back together to continue the discussion.

A search on the internet reveals the majority of the resistance to the vaccine by conservatives is directed toward a government-mandated vaccination program as a requirement for entry into a public school. The decision of whether to vaccinate a minor against this or other sexually transmitted infections should remain with the child's parents or guardian. Also, according to Johns Hopkins researchers:

A new study of survey data finds that only a minority of parents choose not to immunize their children against the sexually transmitted human papillomavirus (HPV) due to concerns that vaccination would encourage or support youth sexual activity, a reason frequently cited by doctors as a barrier to advocating for this vaccine. Instead, the results show, parental concerns that steer young people away from vaccination tend to focus on safety worries, lack of necessity, knowledge about HPV and absence of physician recommendation.[177]

With this information, the Christian can go back to the arguer

---

177 Johns Hopkins Medicine, "The HPV Vaccine: Why Parents Really Choose to Refuse," *Newsroom*, October 24, 2018, https://www.hopkins-medicine.org/news/newsroom/news-releases/the-hpv-vaccine-why-parents-really-choose-to-refuse.

at the agreed-upon time and ask, "Have you ever given any thought to the idea that the objection to the vaccine may not be as you suggested but is an objection to a government-mandated program that requires children to get the vaccine before they are allowed to enter school?" The Christian could then share the information he gathered from the internet and point out to the arguer that his statement that the moral teachings of the Bible ignore and contribute to the sufferings of many people is not a sound conclusion based on the evidence he has provided.

Referring to his argument, Harris uses the conclusion of his ad hominem attack as a premise for a false dilemma.

Premise 1: One of the most pernicious effects of religion is that it tends to divorce morality from the reality of human suffering.

Conclusion: This explains why you Christians are more concerned about human embryos than about the lifesaving promise of stem-cell research.

Harris is offering two options in his conclusion: the Christian is either concerned about human embryos or the life-saving value of stem-cell research. There is, however, a third option that the Christian should point out in response by asking the following question: "Have you given any thought to the life-saving value of umbilical cord stem-cell research?" The Christian can then share information he has discovered about umbilical cord stem cells. For example, Louis A. Cona[178] writes:

> Umbilical cord tissue contains millions of undifferentiated live cells that have immense healing potential. The tissue found inside donated umbilical cords is called Wharton's Jelly and contains millions of youthful, undifferentiated stem cells. Stem cells are grown in a cell media culture, which allows the cells to replicate and produce higher numbers over a few generations; this is called cell expansion. This process can turn a few million stem cells into billions, ready for use in treatments[179].

Umbilical cord stem-cell research is the third alternative. By responding this way, the Christian has, once again, pointed out the error in Harris's argument. The Christian does not have to choose between saving human embryonic stem cells or the life-saving potential of stem-cell research.

---

178   Dr. Cona has been performing stem cell therapy for over ten years. He is a member of the World Academy of Anti-Aging Medicine (WAAAM). He is also a recognized member of the British Medical Association, the General Medical Council (UK), the Caribbean College of Family Physicians, and the American Academy of Family Physicians. He is the medical director for DVC Stem, a world-renowned stem cell therapy clinic located in Grand Cayman.
179   Louis A. Cona, "5 myths about stem cells debunked," *DVCStem*, accessed online December 28, 2020, https://www.dvcstem.com/post/5-myths-about-stem-cells.

Referring to his argument once again, Harris uses the conclusion of his ad hominem attack as a premise for an appeal to pity.

> Premise 1: One of the most pernicious effects of religion is that it tends to divorce morality from the reality of human suffering.
>
> Conclusion: This explains why you Christians can preach against condom use in Sub-Saharan Africa while millions die from AIDS there each year.

The response of the Christian should be to ask the question, "Can you explain what you mean about Christians preaching against condom use, and how did you come to the conclusion that their preaching has led to the death of millions of people from AIDS?" Harris is attempting to place the blame on the Christians' approach to sex education of teaching only abstinence. His explanation is that "We know beyond any doubt, that teaching abstinence alone is not a good way to curb teen pregnancy or the spread of sexually transmitted disease."[180] The Christian's response should be, "Whether or not condom use is included in the abstinence-only education does not change the truth that the moral guidelines for sexual conduct provided in the Bible, if adhered to, will prevent the spread of

---

180 Harris, *Letter*, 27.

AIDS."

In an October 10, 2019, article for the *Washington Times* titled "STD surge shows national need for the Bible," author Cheryl K. Chumley writes:

> But here's the real truth, the elephant in the room truth, the one nobody wants to talk about because it would seem intolerant, or judgmental, or too out-of-touch and rigid for a modern, free and easy world: Sex isn't a need—not like eating and breathing, anyway. So those who choose to have sex should either do so for the purposes sex was intended by God, else face the consequences. And hey now, guess what, drumroll please, consequences for sinful sex include STDs.
>
> Read the Bible. See for yourself. Galatians 6. Romans 1. A little Proverbs 30 thrown in for good measure. And more.
>
> The surge in STDs shows the need for this nation to return to the Bible. It's not a popular message for a growing secular world. But it is the one message that could actually and ultimately cure the country's entire STD problem. For good.[181]

At this point, the Christian could share with Harris that he is correct in his belief that teaching abstinence alone is not

---

181 Cheryl K. Chumley, "STD surge shows national need for the Bible," *Washington Times*, October 10, 2019, https://www.washingtontimes.com/news/2019/oct/10/std-surge-shows-national-need-for-the-bible/.

enough; the reason for abstinence must also be included. Teaching the "Thou shall not…" needs to be coupled with the reason behind the statement. In the Bible, abstinence is referred to as avoiding sexual immorality. In respect to the sacred essence of reproduction, Scripture advises man to refrain from non-marital sexual relations. In this regard, man honors the sanctity of bringing life into the world and even improve the intimate moments with the life partner with whom God has blessed man. More than that, the Christian could use Ephesians 5:3 as a support text for his belief that abstinence is the right and proper approach to pre-marital sex for those who are in a relationship with a Holy God.

Ephesians 5:3, "But immorality or any impurity or greed must not even be named among you, as is proper among saints."

The word "immorality" in this verse comes from the Greek noun *porneia* and carries the meaning of "illicit sexual intercourse, adultery, fornication, homosexuality, lesbianism, intercourse with animals, and sexual intercourse with close relatives."[182] In commenting on this passage, Charles Hodge writes:

Not only fornication, but everything of the same nature, or that leads to it, is to be avoided—and not only avoided, but

182 Strong, *Enhanced Strong's Lexicon.*

not even named among believers. The inconsistency of all such sins with the character of Christians, as saints, men selected from the world and consecrated to God, is such as should forbid the very mention of them in a Christian society.[183]

A person making a claim such as the one made by Harris might at this time say, "Well, that might be fine for those who claim to be Christian, but not everyone in the world is Christian." In making such a statement, the arguer has just refuted his own argument. Now the door has been opened for sharing more of the truth of the gospel, which is the goal of responding to fallacious arguments raised against the Christian worldview.

---

183 Charles Hodge, *Commentary on Ephesians*, electronic ed. (Simpsonville: Christian Classics Foundation, 1996), 283.

Chapter 17

SUMMARY

———

O ne example from each of the twelve logical fallacies encountered by this writer when sharing the gospel has been presented along with a response that demonstrates gentleness and reverence towards the one presenting the argument. The purpose of providing these examples is to demonstrate the need for the development of a discipleship training program that includes a detailed study of Scripture, theology, Christian ethics, and critical thinking. Critical thinking is the connecting link between the Bible, theology, and ethics. It guides believers in making decisions in life based upon the truth of God's Word, especially in a culture hostile to the gospel.

Only twelve logical fallacies were discussed, but according to the "Master List of Logical Fallacies,[184]" developed by Owen Williamson at the University of Texas at El Paso, there are at least 146 logical fallacies. McDurmon states:

184 Owen M. Williamson, "Master List of Logical Fallacies," accessed online November 4, 2020, http://cf.linnbenton.edu/artcom/english/traskd/upload/Master%20List%20of%20Logical%20Fallacies.pdf.

New material bombards us from every outlet every day; a new batch of fallacies passes under the editor's eye or across a producer's screen and into the public every minute. Much of what authors and editors should have tossed in a waste bin, and what news producers should have left on the cutting room floor nevertheless gets published, leaving your mind and your critical thinking ability as the last filter of your soul. You, as an honest Jane or Joe, responsible before God, must discern truth from error, fact from fallacy.[185]

This is the reason for the need of continued training in the skills of critical thinking and where the average church's discipleship training program is falling short. We are not properly preparing Christians to meet the challenges presented by a world that is hostile to the biblical worldview.

In surveying the websites of churches across the United States, very few were found to offer courses in apologetics, critical thinking, or theology in their discipleship training programs. Most courses were focused on the basics: living the Christian life, marriage, parenting, money management, witnessing, and studying books of the Bible. This is understandable since most of the discipleship training materials available for purchase are written to cover these topics. But there are materials available to train Christians in apologetics, critical

---

185 McDurmon, *Biblical Logic*, 19.

thinking, and theology. Listed below are a few websites that offer materials in these areas.

- crossexamined.org
- str.org (Stand to Reason Ministries)
- reasons.org (Reasons to Believe Ministries)
- coldcasechristianity.com
- thechristianworldview.org

BIBLIOGRAPHY

Allen, Blaine A. "Assessing Contemporary Moral Issues From a Biblical-Theological Perspective at Faith Baptist Church, Starkville, Mississippi." Doctor of Ministry Project, New Orleans Baptist Theological Seminary, 1994.

Anderson, Scott. "Attempting to Restore the Christian Story in a Culture of Collapse by Utilizing and Appropriate Apologetic Catechism." Doctor of Ministry Project, Ashland Theological Seminary, 2007.

Andrews, Edward D. *Christian Apologetic Evangelism: Reaching Hearts with the Art of Persuasion.* Cambridge, OH: Christian Publishing House, 2017.

Austin, Michael W. "Anti-Intellectualism in the Church." *Christian Research Journal 39,* no. 4 (2016): 18–23.

Ballard, Mark H., and Timothy K. Christian. *Words Matter: What Is The Gospel?* Bennington: Northeastern Baptist Press, 2020.

Bancroft, Emery H. *Christian Theology: Systematic and Biblical.* Grand Rapids: Zondervan Publishing, 1955.

Barker, Dan. *God: The Most Unpleasant Character In All Fiction.* New York: Sterling Publishing, 2016.

Barna, George. *Think Like Jesus: Make the Right Decision Every Time.* Nashville: Thomas Nelson, 2003.

Beckwith, Francis, William Lane Craig, and J. P. Moreland, eds. To Everyone An Answer: A Case for the Christian Worldview. Downers Grove: IVP Academic, 2004.

Boa, Kenneth D., and Robert M. Bowman Jr. *Faith Has Its Reasons: Integrative Approaches to Defending the Christian Faith.* Colorado Springs: Biblica Publishing, 2006.

Brittain, David G. "Equipping Church Members to Use Popular Culture as an Apologetic Bridge to Post-Moderns." Doctor of Ministry Project, Southwestern Baptist Theological Seminary, 2004.

Bruce, F. F. *The Book of Acts. The New International Commentary on the New Testament.* Grand Rapids: William B. Eerdmans Publishing Company, 1988.

———. *The Epistle to the Colossians to Philemon and to the Ephesians. The New International Commentary on the*

New Testament. Grand Rapids: William B. Eerdmans Publishing Company, 1984.

Bush, Kenneth W. "Shaping the Future: The Role of the Local Church in Nurturing a Christian Worldview." Doctor of Ministry diss., Reformed Theological Seminary, 2006.

Caner, Ergun Mehmet. *When Worldviews Collide.* Nashville: LiferWay Press, 2005.

Carnell, Edward John. *An Introduction to Christian Apologetics: A Philosophical Defense of the Trinitarian-Theistic Faith.* Grand Rapids: Wm. B. Eerdmans Publishing Company, 1948.

Carson, D. A. The Gagging of God: Christianity Confronts Pluralism. Grand Rapids: Zondervan, 1996.

Copan, Paul. *Is God a Moral Monster? Making Sense of the Old Testament God.* Grand Rapids: BakerBooks, 2011.

———. *True For You, But Not For Me: Overcoming Objections to Christian Faith.* Minneapolis: Bethany House, 2009.

———, and Matthew Flannagan. D*id God Really Command Genocide? Coming to Terms with the Justice of God.* Grand Rapids: BakerBooks, 2014.

————, and William Lane Craig, eds. Come Let Us Reason Together: New Essays in Christian Apologetics. Nashville: B & H Academic, 2012.

Craig, William Lane. *On Guard: Defending Your Faith with Reason and Precision.* Colorado Springs: David C. Cook, 2010.

Cullmann, Oscar. *The Earliest Christian Confessions.* Eugene: Wipf and Stock Publishers. 1949.

Davids, Peter H. *The First Epistle of Peter. The New International Commentary on the New Testament.* Grand Rapids: William B. Eerdmans Publishing Company, 1990.

Davis, Stephen T. *God, Reason & Theistic Proofs.* Grand Rapids: William B. Eerdmans Publishing Company, 1997.

Davis, Steven Brent. "Pastoral Perceptions of Critical Thinking in the Process of Discipleship in the Local Church." EdD diss., The Southern Baptist Theological Seminary, 2002.

Dembski, William A. and Michael R. Licona, eds. *Evidence for God: 50 Arguments for Faith from the Bible, History, Philosophy, and Science.* Grand Rapids: Baker Books, 2010.

Dockery, David S., and Trevin K. Wax. Christian Worldview

Handbook. Nashville: Holman, 2019.

Dulles, Avery Cardinal. *A History of Apologetics.* San Francisco: Ignatius Press, 1999.

Durston, Kirk. "The Incompatibility of God and Gratuitous Evil: Implications for the Termination of Civilizations," *Religious Studies* 51, no. 3 (September 2015): 411–419.

Edwards, James R. Romans. *New International Biblical Commentary,* vol. 6. Peabody: Hendrickson Publishers, 1992.

Evans, William. *The Great Doctrines of the Bible.* Chicago: Moody Press, 1974.

Fee, Gordon D. *1 and 2 Timothy, Titus. New International Biblical Commentary*, vol. 13. Peabody: Hendrickson Publishers, 1988.

———. *The First Epistle to the Corinthians. The New International Commentary on the New Testament.* Grand Rapids: William B. Eerdmans Publishing Company, 1987.

Feinberg, John S. *The Many Faces of Evil: Theological Systems and the Problems of Evil.* Wheaton: Crossway Books, 2004.

Ferguson, Terry A. "Worldview and Worship: Forming,

Developing, Practicing, and Proclaiming the Heart of the Story at University Christian Church." DMIN Project, Trinity International University, 2008.

Fernandez, Luly. "Exploring Undergraduate Critical Thinking Dispositions and Use of Critical Thinking Within the Fieldwork Requirement of a Religious and Pastoral Studies Program." PhD diss., Capella University, 2010.

Fernando, Ajith. *Deuteronomy: Loving Obedience to a Loving God. Preaching the Word.* Wheaton: Crossway, 2012.

Frame, John M. *Apologetics to the Glory of God: An Introduction.* Phillipsburg: P & R Publishing, 1994.

Gaven, Greg M. "Equipping a Selected Group of Christians of Pine Grove Baptist Church, Ellisville, Mississippi, to Share Christ With Friends Who Have a Non-Christian Worldview." Doctor of Ministry Project, New Orleans Baptist Theological Seminary, 2006.

Geisler, David and Norman Geisler. *Conversational Evangelism: Connecting with People to Share Jesus.* Eugene: Harvest House Publishers, 2009.

Geisler, Norman L., and Frank Turek. *I Don't Have Enough Faith to Be an Atheist.* Wheaton: Crossway, 2004.

————, and Ronald M. Brooks. *Come, Let Us Reason: An Introduction to Logical Thinking*. Grand Rapids: Baker Academic, 1990.

Glasscock, Ed. Matthew. *Moody Gospel Commentary*. Chicago: Moody Press, 1997.

Gould, Paul M. *Cultural Apologetics: Renewing the Christian Voice, Conscience, and Imagination in a Disenchanted World*. Grand Rapids: Zondervan, 2019.

————, Travis Dickinson and R. Keith Loftin. *Stand Firm: Apologetics and the Brilliance of the Gospel*. Nashville: B & H Academic, 2018.

Green, Michael. *Evangelism in the Early Church*. Grand Rapids: William B. Eerdmans Publishing Company, 2003.

Groothuis, Douglas. *Christian Apologetics: A Comprehensive Case for Biblical Faith*. Downers Grove: IVP Academic, 2011.

Guthrie, George H. *2 Corinthians. Baker Exegetical Commentary on the New Testament*. Grand Rapids: Baker Academic, 2015.

Haber, Jonathan. *Critical Thinking. Cambridge,* MA: The MIT Press, 2020.

Habermas, Gary R. and Michael R. Licona. *The Case for the Resurrection of Jesus*. Grand Rapids: Kregel Publications, 2004.

Halverson, Dean C. *The Compact Guide to World Religions*. Minneapolis: Bethany House, 1996.

Hansen, Walter G. *Galatians. The IVP New Testament Commentary Series,* vol. 9. Downers Grove: IVP Academic, 1994.

Harris, Sam. *Letter to a Christian Nation.* New York: Vintage Books, 2006.

————. *The End of Faith: Religion, Terror, and the Future of Reason.* New York: W. W. Norton & Company, 2004.

Henry, Carl F. H. *The Christian Mindset in a Secular Society: Promoting Evangelical Renewal & National Righteousness.* Portland: Multnomah Press, 1984.

Higham, Terry. *The God Debate: Dawkins in Denial.* Self-published, 2018.

Hillyer, Norman. *1 and 2 Peter, Jude. New International Biblical Commentary,* vol. 16. Peabody: Hendrickson Publishers, 1992.

Hitchens, Christopher. *God Is Not Great: How Religion*

Poisons Everything. New York: Twelve Publishing, 2007.

———, Richard Dawkins, Sam Harris, and Daniel Dennett. *The Four Horsemen*. New York: Random House, 2019.

Hodge, Charles. *Romans. The Crossway Classic Commentaries*. Wheaton: Crossway Books, 1993.

House, H. Wayne. *The Evangelical Dictionary of World Religions*. Grand Rapids: BakerBooks, 2018.

Howard-Snyder, Daniel, ed. *The Evidential Argument from Evil*. Bloomington: Indiana University Press, 1996.

Hughes, William, Jonathan Lavery, and Katheryn Doran. *Critical Thinking: An Introduction to the Basic Skills*. Ontario: Broadview Press, 2015.

James, David B. "Equipping and Preparing High School Students at First Baptist Church, Benton, Arkansas, to Enter the Collegiate Experience with a Christian Worldview." Doctor of Ministry Project, Midwestern Baptist Theological Seminary, 2006.

Janaro, David H. "Equipping Selected Members of Fairfax First Baptist Church, Fairfax, South Carolina, with Essential Christian Apologetic Skills to Engage Jehovah's Witnesses." Doctor of Ministry Project, New Orleans Baptist

Theological Seminary, 2017.

Jensen, Irving L. Jensen's *Survey of the New Testament.* Chicago: Moody Press, 1977.

———. Jensen's *Survey of the Old Testament.* Chicago: Moody Press, 1975.

Jervis, L. Ann. *Galatians. New International Biblical Commentary.* Peabody: Hendrickson Publishers, 1999.

Johnson, Harold. "The Research and Development of a Storying Model to Address the Post-Modern Worldview with the Biblical Worldview." Doctor of Ministry Project, New Orleans Baptist Theological Seminary, 2000.

Keltz, Kyle B., and Tricia Scribner, eds. *Answering the Music Man: Dan Barker's Arguments against Christianity.* Eugene: Wipf & Stock, 2020.

Koukl, Gregory. *Tactics: A Game Plan for Discussing Your Christian Convictions.* Grand Rapids: 2009.

Lennon, Nancy K. "How Professors Infuse Critical Thinking Into College Courses." EdD diss., Seton Hall University, 2014.

Lennox, John C. God's *Undertaker: Has Science Buried God?* Oxford: Lion, 2009.

Luther, Martin. *Commentary on Romans.* Grand Rapids: Zondervan, 1954.

Markos, Louis. *Apologetics for the 21st Century.* Wheaton: Crossway, 2010.

McCallum, Dennis. *Christianity: The Faith That Makes Sense.* Wheaton: Tyndale House Publishers, 1992.

McDurmon, Joel. *Biblical Logic in Theory & Practice.* Powder Springs: American Vision Press, 2015.

Moreland, J. P. *Love Your God With All Your Mind: The Role of Reason in the Life of the Soul.* Colorado Springs: Nav-Press, 2012.
———. *Scientism and Secularism: Learning to Respond to a Dangerous Ideology.* Wheaton: Crossway, 2018.

———, and William Lane Craig, eds. *Philosophical Foundations for a Christian Worldview.* Downers Grove: IVP Academic, 2003.

Morris, Leon. *The First and Second Epistles to the Thessalonians. The New International Commentary on the New Testament.* Grand Rapids: William B. Eerdmans Publishing Company, 1959.

Mounce, Robert H. Matthew. *New International Biblical*

Commentary, vol. 1. Peabody: Hendrickson Publishers, 1991.

Mounce, William D. P*astoral Epistles. Word Biblical Commentary,* vol. 46. Nashville: Thomas Nelson Publishers, 2000.

Murray, John. *The Epistle to the Romans. The New International Commentary on the New Testament.* Grand Rapids: William B. Eerdmans Publishing Company, 1965.

Murray, Michael J., ed. *Reason for the Hope Within.* Grand Rapids: William B. Eerdmans Publishing Company, 1999.

Nash, Ronald H. *Faith & Reason: Searching for a Rational Faith.* Grand Rapids: Zondervan Publishing House, 1988.

Naugle, David K. *Worldview: The History of a Concept.* Grand Rapids: William B. Eerdmans Publishing Company, 2002.

Navabi, Armin. *Why There Is No God: Simple Responses to 20 Common Arguments for the Existence of God.* CreateSpace Independent Publishing Platform, 2014.

Newman, Randy. *Unlikely Converts: Improbable Stories of Faith and What They Teach Us About Evangelism.* Grand Rapids: Kregel Publications, 2019.

Olson, Todd, W. "Preaching in Genesis 1–11 at the Evangelical

Free Church of Wilmar: A Meta-Narrative Foundation for Worldview Formation." Doctor of Ministry Project, Trinity International University, 2004.

Onstott, Jodell. YHWH Exists, vol. 1. Baton Rouge: Emmanuel Publishing, 2014.

Osborne, William R. "Thinking Critically, Reading Faithfully: Critical Biblical Scholarship in the Christian Classroom." Criswell Theological Review 11, no.2 (Spring 2014): 79–89.

Park, Sin Yong. "Developing a Critical Thinking Program for Small Group Leaders in Cornerstone Korean Church, Elgin, Illinois." DMIN Project, The Southern Baptist Theological Seminary, 2017.

Partridge, Christopher. *Introduction to World Religions.* Minneapolis: Fortress Press, 2018.

Patzia, Arthur G. *Ephesians, Colossians, Philemon. New International Biblical Commentary*, vol. 10. Peabody: Hendrickson Publishers, 1990.

Plantinga, Alvin. *God, Freedom, and Evil.* Grand Rapids: William B. Eerdmans Publishing Company, 1974.

Ryrie, C. Charles. *Basic Theology: A Popular Systematic*

Guide to Understanding Biblical Truth. Chicago: Victor Books, 1984.

Sanders, Don. "From Critical Thinking to Spiritual Maturity: Connecting the Apostle Paul and John Dewey." Christian Education Journal 15, no. 1 (April 2018): 90–104.

Schaeffer, Francis A. *The God Who Is There*. Downers Grove: IVP Books, 1982.

Scott, James M. *2 Corinthians. New International Biblical Commentary,* vol. 8. Peabody: Hendrickson Publishers, 1998.

Sell, Alan P. F. *Confessing and Commending the Faith: Prolegomena to Christian Apologetics.* Eugene: Wipf & Stock Publishers, 2002.

Shepardson, Andrew I. *Who's Afraid of the Unmoved Mover? Postmodernism and Natural Theology.* Eugene: Pickwick Publications, 2019.

Shirley, Christopher Jay. "Let's Be Reasonable: An Integrative Discipleship Book Preparing Christians to Give a Reason for the Hope Within Through a Study of Biblical Theology, Worldviews, and Apologetics." DMIN diss., Southwestern Baptist Theological Seminary, 2012.

Sire, James W. *Why Good Arguments Often Fail: Making a More Persuasive Case for Christ*. Downers Grove: Inter-Varsity Press, 2006.

————. *The Universe Next Door: A Basic Worldview Catalog*. Downers Grove: InterVarsity Press, 2004.

————. *Discipleship of the Mind: Learning to Love God in the Ways We Think*. Downers Grove: InterVarsity Press, 1990.

Smith, Christian and Melinda Lundquist Denton. *Soul Searching; The Religious and Spiritual Lives of American Teenagers*. New York: Oxford University Press, 2005.

Smith, Gary V. *Isaiah 1–39. The New American Commentary*, vol. 15a. Nashville: B&H Publishing Group, 2007.

Soards, Marion L. *1 Corinthians. New International Biblical Commentary*, vol.7. Peabody: Hendrickson Publishers, 1999.

Sommerfeld, Scott G. "Preparing Thinking Christians to Survive and Thrive in a Culture of Choice." Doctor of Ministry Project, Concordia Seminary, 2007.

Son, Jeong We. "Critical Thinking and Church Education." Korean Journal of Christian Studies 60 (December 2008):

177–195.

Staton, Knofel. *Timothy-Philemon. Unlocking the Scriptures for You.* Cincinnati: Standard Publishing, 1984.

Sunshine, Glenn S. *Why You Think The Way You Do: The Story of Western Worldviews From Rome to Home.* Grand Rapids: Zondervan, 2009.

Sweis, Khaldoun A. and Chad V. Meister, eds. *Christian Apologetics: An Anthology of Primary Sources.* Grand Rapids: Zondervan, 2012.

Trau, Jane Mary. "Fallacies in the Argument from Gratuitous Suffering," The New Scholasticism 60 (Fall 1986): 485–489.

Vine, W. E. *Vine's Expository Commentary on 1 & 2 Thessalonians.* Nashville: Thomas Nelson Publishers, 1997.

Virkler, Henry A. *A Christian's Guide to Critical Thinking.* Eugene: Wipf & Stock, 2005.

Wainwright, *William. Philosophy of Religion.* Belmont: Wadsworth Pub. Co., 1999.

Warren, Jeffrey L. "Training Youth Workers to Teach Youth Basic Christian Apologetics." DMIN Project, Southwestern Baptist Theological Seminary, 1995.

Weston, Anthony. *A Rulebook for Arguments.* Indianapolis: Hackett Publishing Company, 2009.

Williams, David J. *1 and 2 Thessalonians. New International Biblical Commentary*, vol. 12. Peabody: Hendrickson Publishers, 1992.

———. *Acts. New International Commentary*, vol. 5. Peabody: Hendrickson Publishers, 1990.

Winkler, Charles L. "Fishers of Men for the 21st Century: Training Lay Evangelists to Reach Post-Modern Man." Doctor of Ministry Project, Westminster Theological Seminary, 2004.

Wright, Christopher J. H. *Deuteronomy. Understanding the Bible Commentary Series*. Grand Rapids: BakerBooks, 1996.

———. *Deuteronomy. New International Biblical Commentary*, vol. 4. Peabody: Hendrickson Publishers, 1996.

Zacharias, Ravi. *Beyond Opinion: Living the Faith We Defend.* Nashville: Thomas Nelson, 2007.

———. *The Logic of God: 52 Christian Essentials for the Heart and Mind.* Grand Rapids: Zondervan, 2019.

Zodhiates, *Spiros. The Complete Word Study Dictionary: New Testament.* Chattanooga: AMG Publishers, 1993.

CPSIA information can be obtained
at www.ICGtesting.com
Printed in the USA
LVHW082046240222
711939LV00012B/421